CONTENTS

Chapter One: Coping at Work

Chapter Two: Young People and Work

Chapter Three: Work and the Family

Introduction

The Work Revolution is the twenty-fifth volume in the series: **Issues**. The aim of this series is to offer up-to-date information about important issues in our world.

The Work Revolution looks at changes in the way we work and how they are effecting the individual, young people and the family.

The information comes from a wide variety of sources and includes:
Government reports and statistics
Newspaper reports and features
Magazine articles and surveys
Literature from lobby groups
and charitable organisations.

It is hoped that, as you read about the many aspects of the issues explored in this book, you will critically evaluate the information presented. It is important that you decide whether you are being presented with facts or opinions. Does the writer give a biased or an unbiased report? If an opinion is being expressed, do you agree with the writer?

The Work Revolution offers a useful starting-point for those who need convenient access to information about the many issues involved. However, it is only a starting-point. At the back of the book is a list of organisations which you may want to contact for further information.

*****

I have seen the future and it doesn't work

Are you ready for the future? A world of cyberspace conferences, e-mail memos, technological elites and down-trodden service workers. Jobs as we know them are finished, says Helen Jones

Welcome to the future. A world with an underclass of technological have-nots, filled with rage and frustration, and a small elite group of 'knowledge workers' who work from home because it's too dangerous to venture out. Science fiction? Possibly. But professional futurologists believe that work will change beyond recognition in the next 20 years.

'The changing shape of the world of work will have a huge impact on jobs of the future, with new roles being created and existing ones obsolete,' says Anna Reed, a researcher for Reed Personnel Services.

'In some areas, demand will grow. Genetic engineers will become more common as public disquiet dies down and the advantages of the technology become clear. Other roles will expand, so that secretaries will routinely organise virtual conferences over the Internet and travel agents will include trips to the moon,' she says.

So how can you future-proof your career? Should you take a job in computer technology rather than in the City or become a health care worker rather than an estate agent?

Richard Holt, a director of consultancy Business Strategies, says: 'It's very difficult to predict the jobs of the future and those which will no longer be needed, but management and information technology skills look like the best combination.'

In a report called *Occupations in the Future*, Holt's company predicts that there will be a growth in a number of different areas: 'Back in 1981 there were nearly six million people employed in manufacturing and only two and a half million in financial and business services. The two are now equal, at a little over four million. Public services, however, continue to be the largest growth sector and by 2006 may account for the employment of over eight million people,' says Mr Holt.

He also believes that service industries will be a major source of employment. 'The fastest growth from now until 2006 is likely to occur in services such as restaurant and bar staff, with over 35,000 jobs being created.'

Paul Edwards, chairman of the Henley Centre for Forecasting, agrees. 'Anything that is service-oriented will be in demand, whether it's for gardeners, cleaners, nannies or somebody to walk your dog.'

Marian Salzman, a futurologist and head of Brand Futures at advertising agency Young & Rubicam in New York, says that stressed-out executives will want to use the services of oxygen bars where they can get invigorating shots of pure air and will also seek solitude from faxes, e-mail and the Internet at resorts where they can unwind.

But service industry jobs will not only offer greater convenience to consumers, they will also provide human interaction.

'Personal trainers, silver service waiting staff and party organisers will be in demand. As work becomes an exercise in cyberspace, it is jobs which provide human contact which may grow fastest,' says Anna Reed.

However, service industry jobs are usually poorly paid. How do you ensure that you are one of the elite group who can afford to employ this army of cleaners, masseurs and dog walkers to help with your frantic life?

Specialise. Futurologists at BT suggest that genetic engineers, biological scientists and tele-communications and information technologists will be in great demand as will doctors and other health care professionals. Food technologists who can produce 'nutraceuticals' – foods which contain all the nutrients we need and have medicinal benefits – may also be popular.

But a flexible attitude is equally important. Management guru Charles Handly believes that the future is freelance. Workers will build up packages of jobs working for a

'People have to understand that there is no such thing as a job for life any more and it is no longer a bad thing to move quickly from job to job

number of companies and their loyalty will be to themselves rather than to a single employer. As a result,

employment agencies specialising in finding short-term contracts are likely to be a growth industry.

And Graham Whitehead, a futurologist at BT, says that, although jobs will not disappear overnight, some will gradually become obsolete.

'People have to understand that there is no such thing as a job for life any more and it is no longer a bad thing to move quickly from job to job. Keep moving, be flexible and adaptable or you may find you don't have a future,' he says.

First published in The Independent May, 1998

The workplace revolution

When Cardinal Hume yesterday denounced the impact of long hours, he touched on a social transformation. Here we examine the crisis of modern working life

Kiss goodbye to the nine-to-five job for life; embrace the flexible split-shift family of 'portfolio' workers of the future.

That has been the refrain of politicians and pundits alike, as the transformation of work has acceler-ated over the past two decades.

Women's employment has risen dramatically, industrial and manu-facturing jobs have been pro-gressively scythed, self-employment and 'flexible' working have mush-roomed as traditional careers and apprenticeships have been swept away.

More of the British population is now in some form of work than in almost any other European country. But the jobs available have become less secure, undermined by casualisa-tion, chronic mass unemployment and the long retreat of the trade unions. Millions of older people have been forced out of the labour market, the gap between pay rates has widened sharply and power at the workplace has passed unequivocally upwards.

Technology and globalisation have created opportunities for some, or enforced idleness for others. The same goes for the rise of part-time working and self-employment. Evidence of job-related stress and

By Seumas Milne and Larry Elliott

bullying is growing, as competitive and profit-driven pressures take their toll in the workplace.

For the most part, the pro-liferation of casual work and greater freedom of hire-and-fire for employers has not been reflected in greater flexibility for employees.

Tony Blair's government regards

cutting the dole queues as one of its central tasks. But a growing body of evidence shows that another, apparently contradictory problem – that of overwork – is escalating and eating into social and family life. Longer working hours, evening and weekend working are spreading, preying ever more on domestic and child time and adding to the sense of a crisis of working life.

At one end of the scale, pro-fessionals are spending more evenings and weekends in the office or hunched over a laptop in an effort to meet the demands of greater competi-tion, fewer staff and the 'long hours culture' associated with managerial promotion. At the other, as manual workers' wages have been squeezed, low-income families are having to do more overtime or double up jobs. There are now 1.2 million people with two jobs – two-thirds of them women – almost twice the number in 1984.

British workers work by far the longest hours in the European Union – with a third doing more than a 48-hour week – and the UK is the only country where the average working week has lengthened in the past decade. New research by Susan Harkness, of the Centre for Eco-nomic Performance at the London

School of Economics, found that is mainly because of extra paid and unpaid overtime.

Since 1988, the average number of hours of overtime worked by full-time males has increased from four to seven, and for women from three to six.

One in six employees now works during the evening, with the greatest rise in anti-social working in the 1990s in sales and professional occupations. One in two working men and one in three working women work some or most Sundays.

In one in four two-parent households, at least one parent now regularly works in the evening. Women with children in two-parent families are 50 per cent more likely to work evenings than those without, due to the high cost of child care or, increasingly, a partner out of work.

Only 51 per cent of employed men and 38 per cent of employed women now work full time for five days a week, with no regular evening or night work. Over 45 per cent of women employees work more than 40 hours a week and 10 per cent over 50 hours, compared with 27 per cent and 4 per cent respectively in the late 1980s.

This increasingly lop-sided distribution of work and free time has given rise to the idea of the 'work-rich' and 'work-poor': where 40 per cent of those aged 50-65 are not working and one in five children live in workless households; while the better-off work-rich are so time-poor they now employ an army of low-paid workers – from cleaners and nannies to pizza-delivery bikers – to service them.

The latest to denounce the impact of long working hours is the leader of Britain's Catholics, Cardinal Basil Hume, who yesterday raged against the impact on children and said that shopworkers and City traders preparing for the euro should have refused to work over Christmas. He was joined by the new Anglican Bishop of Liverpool, James Jones, in accusing employers of putting profits before people. Both churchmen were criticised by Ruth Lea of the Institute of Directors for being out of touch. 'Businesses have to compete,' she said.

The Government hopes its Fairness at Work and European Working Time legislation will help right the balance – although the impact is likely to be modest.

British workers work by far the longest hours in the European Union – with a third doing more than a 48-hour week

---

Meanwhile, 'highly selective media myths' about women conquering the commanding heights of the economy are under attack in a new book about women in the workplace, *Having None of It* by Suzanne Franks. The feminisation of work, she argues, has meant 'armies of low-paid women in service industries. For the vast majority of women, work has not brought "liberation"; they work in segregated, low-paid, part-time jobs, because average families need a second wage.'

Others have challenged the view that changes to the labour market have resulted in higher levels of job insecurity. William Walde-grave, the former Tory minister, has claimed job insecurity is largely a psychological phenomenon, as the length of job tenure has changed relatively little in the past two decades.

But the Organisation for Economic Cooperation and Development takes a different view. As well as depending on job stability, tenure and retention rates, it said in a 1997 report, insecurity also depends on the consequences of 'separation' – such as the ease of obtaining a new job, its characteristics, and the experience of being jobless.

And the evidence suggests the cost of losing a job is now greater than in the post-war period, when most people could be fairly sure of finding a new position on a similar wage fairly quickly, while those unable to find work were protected by relatively generous welfare benefits.

'Insecurity is significantly lower in countries where the unemployment benefit replacement rate is higher, where there is a higher level of collective bargaining and . . . where collective bargaining is more centralised,' the OECD said.

The flexible labour market, in other words, comes at a price.

© *The Guardian January, 1999*

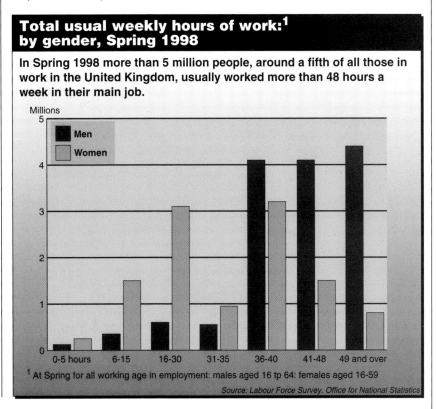

Total usual weekly hours of work:[1] by gender, Spring 1998

In Spring 1998 more than 5 million people, around a fifth of all those in work in the United Kingdom, usually worked more than 48 hours a week in their main job.

Millions

■ Men
☐ Women

0-5 hours | 6-15 | 16-30 | 31-35 | 36-40 | 41-48 | 49 and over

[1] At Spring for all working age in employment: males aged 16 tp 64: females aged 16-59

Source: Labour Force Survey. Office for National Statistics

Can this last?

New research says that the way we work has too high a price and it must change. Roger Trapp and Barrie Clement report

The overwhelming majority of British workers make sacrifices at home for the sake of their careers with half regretting missing their children growing up or putting work before home or family, new research says.

And a separate report for Opportunity 2000, the campaign to promote women in the workforce, shows that almost half of female senior managers have rejected promotion – or failed to apply for it – because of the pressure it would have put on their family relationships.

The larger study, covering male and female employees of various ages and levels of responsibility, also reveals personal sacrifices ranging from divorces and being absent from partners during serious illness to missing school fairs and not spending enough time on leisure or hobbies.

One in ten of the women interviewed said they had postponed or forgone having children for the sake of the job and women were twice as likely as men to have difficulties forming relationships because of their work.

With what the researchers admit were surprising response levels among men, the survey puts renewed pressure on businesses and other organisations to move to break the 'long-hours culture' and introduce new ways of working, or lose the people on whom they depend for future success.

There is already growing evidence that young people at the start of their careers are not prepared to make the sorts of sacrifices that previous generations have made. A much-quoted finding of research among business graduates by the accountants Coopers and Lybrand was that they were prepared to put their personal lives before their careers, while the author

Bruce Tulgan, who is an expert on the so-called Generation X, argues that employers cannot expect such employees to work in the same ways as their predecessors.

Ceridian Performance Partners, the international consultancy specialising in advising employers on these issues, conducted 'the great work/life debate' with the magazine *Management Today*. Liz Bargh, chief executive for the United Kingdom, said: 'The report sends a clear signal – our present way of working is unsustainable, the cost is too high, in human terms and in business terms. Business will have to work with employees to balance work and life for compassion and competitiveness.'

For most people, personal life comes before their career, with only 28 per cent getting most satisfaction from work

---

As she did in her previous role as director of Opportunity 2000, Ms Bargh stresses that there is a 'business case', rather than just a moral reason for change.

The survey of 5,500 people finds that 46 per cent of workers find it hard to meet both their personal and work commitments, with women

suffering most – 61 per cent of them say they have less and less time for themselves. One in three women would take a pay cut in order to gain more time for family life.

For most people, personal life comes before their career, with only 28 per cent getting most satisfaction from work.

Among managers, 67 per cent say they are expected to ask more and more of their staff and 34.5 per cent feel they often push them too hard. And that pressure is taking its toll on organisations – with 32.4 per cent of respondents saying that work/life pressure is a prime cause of staff turnover. The figure is more than 40 per cent for public sector and larger organisations.

And, while only 28.1 per cent of senior managers and directors see workload as a growing factor in staff turnover, 40.5 per cent of middle managers do.

Top of the employees' wish list of things that could make a difference is working fewer hours. This is followed by changing the company culture, working flexible hours, reducing or avoiding commuting, working from home, changing jobs or relocating, getting more staff, earning more, retiring and reducing stress.

The smaller survey for Opportunity 2000, prepared by Ashridge Management College, covered 176 managers representing an equal number of men and women.

Both men and women said that the difficulty of balancing home and work was the biggest problem when accepting a senior appointment.

Some 79 per cent of women felt it was the biggest drawback and 67 per cent of men did so.

However, while one in ten women listed long hours as a reason for rejecting promotion, not one man indicated it was an important issue. And in high-flying couples, more than 43 per cent of women had either rejected promotion or failed to apply for it for fear of damaging their 'dual career' relationships, while only 6 per cent of their male partners had suffered from the same sensitivities.

But Ann Chant, director of Opportunity 2000, believes that attitudes are changing. She points out that the very youngest men are as concerned as their partners that promotion might sour their love lives.

The Ceridian Performance Partners report is available priced £37. Tel: 0181 324 5553.

Manager turned father and porter

Paul Giggle, 47, of Happisburgh in Norfolk used to be in charge of 300 employees in a mechanical engineering factory. He put in at least 60 hours a week and says he had virtually no contact with his two elder children until they were four.

'I hardly saw my children when they were younger. I never changed their nappies, I never fed them, I never got up in the night when they were crying because I was always exhausted from the day's work.

'I had a 45-minute journey each way and two evenings a week and all Saturday afternoon I was playing football as a semi-professional. Basically, I was never there which was awful for the whole family.'

Mr Giggle says his two sons, now 31 and 23, missed out on having a father but he was a slave to the wage.

'You have the mortgage to meet and all your other financial commitments and the overtime paid very well,' he said. 'The only time we would all get together was for Sunday dinner. It didn't only affect my children, it affected me and my first wife.'

Although he remarried, Mr Giggle's life did not change. 'My stepdaughter was probably the only three-year-old able to order an Indian takeaway. My second wife, Debbie, also had a very demanding job so we ended up eating out six nights a week.'

It was not until his son Charlie was born five years ago that Mr Giggle

The survey puts renewed pressure on businesses and other organisations to move to break the 'long-hours culture' and introduce new ways of working

decided to have a radical work-life change.

'Even before Debbie became pregnant, we both decided that things had to be different,' he says. 'I wanted to make up for all the things I didn't give to my other sons. I just couldn't bring this baby into the same, pressurised environment.'

In 1992, Giggle took voluntary redundancy and became a house husband. 'It was the best decision I ever made in my life,' he said. 'I had to leave my job because there was no way the company would have been open to flexible working options.'

Now Charlie has turned five,

Mr Giggle works as a night porter, a job which allows him to sleep during the day while his son is at school.

'I don't think I'll ever go back into engineering,' he said. 'It is too pressurised and I don't want to give up what I've got.'

Director helped by nanny and parents

Esther Kaposi, of London, is a 38-year-old mother of two and director of corporate affairs for PowerGen. Although currently on maternity leave with her five-week-old baby, Ms Kaposi intends to go back to work full-time.

On an average working day, Ms Kaposi leaves the house at 8am and returns around 7pm. 'I have a full-time nanny who comes to our house and my parents live nearby which is very helpful,' she said. 'My husband works from home which means his hours are more flexible than mine. It is definitely easier for me to work with two small children than it is for some other mothers.'

Ms Kaposi believes people in senior positions have an easier time balancing their home and work lives because they can tailor the day to suit their own timetable.

'I'm not one of these people who stays at work just to be seen,' she said. 'If I need to do a longer day because of a particular project then I will because it will probably be something that motivates me. But you don't need to work long hours to get on.'

Her fine balancing act is, she says, down to effective time management. 'To be successful I think you need to manage your time well at work and at home. My elder daughter has a sleep in the afternoon and doesn't go to bed until 8pm, so I try to be at home for then. If I'm not home in time I will speak to her on the telephone.

'My situation is not ideal but it is not awful, although I'm always going to remain flexible and keep an open mind about the way I work. I am not going to close off the downshifting option.'

© The Independent
June, 1998

The great life/work debate

The survey

Who we talked to

The sample was drawn from subscribers to *Management Today* as well as members of the Institute of Management, totalling 5,501 responses.

What they said

The picture that emerges is of a workforce where only four in ten are reasonably sure that they have got their life in balance. Many managers appear to be sacrificing their personal life, and that of those close to them, for their work.

We found a majority of managers who are working long, not always justifiable, hours, under increasingly high levels of pressure and who admit that in many cases they are pushing staff too hard.

Further, we found that many organisations appear to be at best unenlightened as to the potentially damaging effects of this imbalance – to their businesses, yet alone their staff – or who appear to have chosen to ignore the situation.

Following is a synopsis of the main findings from the survey:

The actual working week

- Overall, men spend more time at work than do women. Around half of both sexes spend between 41-50 hours at work each week, and 27.8% of men and 18.1% of women are at work for more than 51 hours.
- Private Sector respondents tend to work longer hours than those in the Public Sector.
- Most managers work a five-day week, however, one-fifth routinely work 6 days.
- Long hours are seen to simply go with the job, and at least one-third of respondents have only partial control over their hours.

The ideal working week

- Most managers would prefer a four-day working week with longer hours each day – and would choose Friday as their extra day off.
- Most people would prefer to start work early, and there is little enthusiasm for late working.

Home Life

- Women tend to have most responsibility when it comes to domestic chores.
- Men say that most decisions are shared – but women aren't so sure. Over 4 in 10 women consider that most of the time they alone make the decisions.
- Only half of respondents feel they take their fair share of responsibility on the home front, and they think their family would agree.

Dealing with personal matters

- 3 in 10 respondents frequently have to take time out at work to deal with personal matters – with money matters, healthcare and personal phone calls topping the list.

- Holidays etc. aside, close to half of respondents took no time off for personal reasons in the past year – but when they did, women were far more likely than men to 'go sick'.

Balance in personal life

- A quarter or more say that they would trade pay for more personal time.
- If they had to choose, one-fifth of managers would put their career before their personal life and another one-fifth might.
- Close to half of our respondents are finding it increasingly hard to meet both work and personal commitments – this is particularly so for women.
- 3 in 10 managers get most of their satisfaction in life from their work.
- Only 4 in 10 managers are reasonably happy that their work and personal life balance is about right.

The balance at work

- Over two-thirds of managers say they are expected to ask more and more from their staff, and only one-third would deny that they push staff too hard.
- Only a third of managers say flexible working would reduce efficiency.
- 3 in 10 managers say there are times when they would rather be at work.

Corporate culture matters

- Up to 4 in 10 managers say workload pressure is a prime cause of staff turnover.
- Two-thirds of all managers say working long hours is often confused with commitment, and half of middle managers say that working long hours is more to do with inefficiency than workload.
- Only one-third of respondents say their employer does enough to help staff maintain a healthy work/life balance, and many say their employer's commitment is no more than window dressing.

Sacrifices & wish lists

- Missing children growing and putting work before home life, head the top ten list of personal sacrifices.
- Working fewer hours and changing corporate culture head the Top Ten Wish List for respondents

In their own words

'In my business life I still encounter both men and women who view a balance between work/family as unachievable. If you express the opinion that this is a balance you strive to achieve, you are somehow judged as not taking work seriously and possibly being unable to deliver a premium service.'

Female respondent
31-35 year age group

'I enjoy my job and get a buzz out of working hard to deliver results. I also enjoy spending time with my family. The constant pressure to satisfy both can be a strain. Work is never finished and the family can suffer.'

Male respondent
36-40 year age group

'Every eighteen months or so I face the decision of taking on more work commitments/promotion versus time with my child.'

Female respondent
36-40 year age group

'Where I work there is also a culture of "you must be seen to work late or unsocial hours and weekends to be part of the team" which is very sad.'

Male respondent
36-40 year age group

'I have changed employer twice – and accepted significant salary reductions on both occasions – in order to protect my personal life: first on getting married, and then on having the second of our two children.'

Male respondent
41-50 year age group

- The above is an extract from *The Great Work/Life Debate – The Definitive Summary*, produced by Ceridian Performance Partners and *Management Today*. Ceridian Performance Partners are the leading international provider of corporate work/life consulting and services to major employer organisations throughout the world. They can be contacted at Ceridian Performance Partners, Celcon House, 289-293 High Holborn, London, WC1V 7HU. Fax: 0171 420 3849. *Management Today* is the leading monthly journal circulating to 98,000 general subscribers and members of the Institute of Management. Their address is Management Today, 174 Hammersmith Road, London, W6 7JP. Fax: 0171 413 4138.
To order a copy of *The Great Work/Life Debate – The Definitive Summary*, send a cheque for £37 to Ceridian Performance Partners, Freepost Lon 3590, London W3 6EE (no stamp required if mailing within the UK).

Happy jobless laugh off the German work ethic

By Denis Staunton in Berlin

Workshy of the world unite: you have nothing to lose but your shame. That's the message from a German pressure group, the Happy Unemployed.

While politicians argue about how to get 4 million jobless Germans off the dole, these unemployed Berliners have become crusaders for idleness, arguing that they are doing the state a favour by doing nothing.

Since issuing its manifesto a few weeks ago, the group has received hundreds of letters from unemployed people who fear that an economic upturn could force them back into work. For many, life began the moment they lost their job.

'I've learnt to paint and compose on the synthesiser. I've become creative and go to parties. I need time because I have one girlfriend in Cologne and another in Düsseldorf,' a man from Aachen wrote.

The manifesto, *At Last I Have Time*, argues that the unemployed are cowed by peer pressure into pretending that they want to work.

According to founder Guillaume Paoli, aged 39, the real difficulty unemployed people face is pressure from the authorities to look for work. 'The obligation to work is a big problem.'

He believes the happily unemployed should be rewarded for leaving jobs free for those who enjoy work. He claims that the economy requires a certain level of unemployment to keep inflation low and argues that, since the stock market rewards companies that lay off staff, sacked workers often generate more profit than those who remain employed.

But the authorities show no sign of easing off on the workshy, as an unemployed woman from Koblenz wrote in the group's magazine.

'For the past four years I have been happily out of work, or free of work as I call it,' she wrote. 'Unfortunately, my happiness is disturbed time and again by the employment office.'

Careers turn heat on Cool Britannia

Nick Hopkins on a survey revealing a nation of reluctant workaholics increasingly stressed by the relentless demands of their jobs

It will not come as a surprise to any one heading to work this morning with a heavy heart, but it seems Britain is becoming a nation of reluctant workaholics.

People are working longer hours than before. They are more stressed and are making greater sacrifices for the sake of their careers.

Marriages and relationships are crumbling under the strain. Children are significant losers, too. The workforce spends less and less time at home, and working women are either forgoing having children, or postponing motherhood until there is 'a window of opportunity'.

These are just some of the discouraging findings of a report published today by *Management Today* magazine and Ceridian Performance Partners, a management consultancy which specialises in work/life analysis.

According to their survey – the biggest of its kind – Cool Britannia is overheating. People throughout the country are increasingly putting work before anything else, making decisions and compromises which they later regret.

More than 5,500 readers of the magazine took part, replying to a comprehensive questionnaire which asked pertinent questions about the way they juggle their commitments.

A large majority – 4,615 – said they had sacrificed something important at home for their career. Half said they had missed their children growing up, or been forced to put work before their family.

Others complained that they had had to move house for work, or had seen their social and private lives squeezed into non-existence by career demands. The sacrifices they had made ranged from the irritating, to the plain unforgivable.

Many admitted missing school fairs. Some men had missed the birth of their children. A few volunteered that they had been away when their partner had been seriously ill.

Almost half of the readers said they found it almost impossible to meet both personal and work commitments. Surprisingly, one in four men and one in three women said they would accept a pay cut to improve their situation.

According to the report, the outlook for working women is particularly bleak.

Not only do they feel that men are still not pulling their weight at home, but it appears women make greater sacrifices, and have a tougher time, to achieve modest career goals.

One in 10 had passed up the opportunity to have children for the sake of their job. Working women also find it twice as hard to find partners as working men.

Of the managers who took part, 67 per cent said they were expected to ask more and more of their staff, and 34 per cent felt they often pushed them too hard. More than 30 per cent said work/life pressure was a prime cause of staff leaving. In the public sector and large organisations this figure soared to more than 40 per cent.

However, only one in three managers felt their company was doing all it could to help them maintain a healthy balance between home and working life.

The readers cheered themselves up by drawing up a wish-list of possible solutions to the work/family

conundrum. Their answers were just as telling.

Working fewer hours and changing corporate culture were the top two, followed by more obvious answers like earning more money and changing jobs.

Liz Bargh, Ceridian Performance Partners' chief executive, said the survey had 'hit a nerve in the lives of working people'. She added: 'The number of people who responded was overwhelming. The sacrifices some are making for the sake of their careers are shocking.'

She concluded: 'The report sends a clear signal: our present way of working is unsustainable, the cost is too high in human and business terms. Business will have to work with employees to balance work and life for compassion and for competitiveness.'

Case one

'People who work hard have nothing to be ashamed of.'
Zena Everett, aged 33, set up a recruitment consultancy in Holborn, central London, six years ago. As the firm grew, she found she was working very long hours and weekends. She made sacrifices to pursue her career, but feels the effort was entirely worthwhile.

Miss Everett, who lives in north London, does not regret any of the choices she made, but she is acutely aware that not all her staff share her zeal.

'Perhaps relationships went by the wayside, but I would have continued them if I had wanted to. The fact is, I wanted the business to succeed more than I wanted the relationships to succeed.

'People who work hard have nothing to be ashamed of. I do have a social life, and I am engaged, so I do not feel I have missed out that much, and I do not think that I am abnormal.

'I am in the lucky position that I can now manage my time much better than I used to because the firm is well-established.

'I am well aware of the problems that working too hard can bring to someone's home life. If I think that one of my employees is pushing themselves too hard, I will call them

into my office and ask them why.

'I have made some sacrifices in my personal life, but they were ones I was prepared to make and I do not regret them.'

Case two

Change proves no solution as couple's jobs take over.
Kevin and Eloise Appleby, both aged 32, moved to Bury St Edmunds, Suffolk, from Dorking, Surrey, hoping that a change of jobs and environment would give them more time together.

Married last year, they found that Kevin's work in London as manager of the Wren Orchestra and Eloise's as an events co-ordinator with the National Trust left them little time for themselves. They have been talking about starting a family, too.

When they were both offered middle-management posts at St Edmundsbury borough council, they hoped their lives would become less

---

'Our present way of working is unsustainable, the cost is too high in human and business terms. Business will have to work with employees to balance work and life for compassion and for competitiveness'

---

hectic. Kevin is in charge of the town's annual festival, and Eloise is a tourism manager.

But any thoughts that they were heading for an easier life away from commuter-land quickly evaporated. They were working harder than ever.

'When we lived in Dorking, Kevin often worked seven days a week, which meant we did not have time for our own lives,' said Eloise.

'We moved to Bury St Edmunds to try to give ourselves more space, but we are working just as hard as before. Much of the work is self-inflicted… if you take pride in what you do, sometimes you have to make sacrifices.

'When we left university we managed to have a work and a social life, but nowadays, it takes most of our energy just to keep the work side of things together,' she added.

'We have become parents without having children. We stay in a lot, and don't go out to see our friends that often. At some point we would like to have children, and at the moment we are discussing which one of us will have to stay at home.'

Kevin added: 'It is very much the way of the world. I don't want to whinge about the hours I work, because I get a real buzz out of what I do, but it is really difficult to manage both sides of your life, even when you work for the same employer. I don't think we spend any more time together than we did before.'

© *The Guardian*
June, 1998

Office workers sinking under tide of technology

O ffice workers are being overwhelmed by a deluge of e-mails, phone calls, faxes and other messages as communication technologies leave them with too little time to do their work.

A study by Gallup and the Institute for the Future, published yesterday, found that the average middle-management executive sends or receives 178 messages and documents each day.

Secretarial staff face more than 190 daily correspondences, including post, e-mail, faxes, phone calls, voice-mail, sticky notes, paper messages, courier deliveries and internal mail.

Nancy Ozawa, director of the Institute for the Future, said: 'We have passed the point where communications tools are aiding efficiency. The day is coming when people will lie down in the road and say, "I cannot do this any more"'.

'Initially, technologies such as e-mail make you more productive, but some employees can have up to 100 messages waiting for them every morning so they start to collect their messages before they leave home and their home life suffers.'

Once they get to work, five out of six workers in large companies are interrupted three or more times per hour by messages and more than 71 per cent feel overwhelmed by their correspondence.

'It's become like a badge of honour in some cases. Employees get home and say to their spouses, "I have survived 170 messages today", but then they have to do their actual work at home or at weekends,' Mrs Ozawa said.

The study found that a gridlock is emerging which makes it even harder to get the attention of the recipient. As employees become frustrated at not being able to get through, they send the same message several times by different channels, thus creating even more traffic.

The concept of the paperless

By Robert Uhlig, Technology Correspondent

office remains a pipe-dream. According to the study, most employees regularly use three methods of communication to impart the same message.

> *'We have passed the point where communications tools are aiding efficiency. The day is coming when people will lie down in the road and say, "I cannot do this any more".'*

'Employees will first send an e-mail to a colleague or contact, then print it out and fax it to the same person,' Mrs Ozawa said. 'They then send it by post and, finally, phone to check the recipient has received it.'

One consequence uncovered by the study is a backlash by workers against the expectation that they should be within constant and easy reach of colleagues.

Several employees candidly admitted to switching pagers off, or purposely letting mobile phone batteries run down to limit their communications workload.

Although the study, entitled *Communications Overload*, looked at 1,000 of the largest international companies, it warned that the problems would soon become pervasive in companies of all sizes.

More than 8 in 10 middle-management executives in the survey used e-mail, but now that e-mail use is spreading to smaller companies and to blue-collar workers in larger companies, the overload is expected to become worse.

Meredith Fischer, a vice-president at the office equipment company Pitney Bowes, which commissioned the research, said the solution was for large companies to have a 'mission control' of 'traffic police' who strategically sort and filter information for their colleagues and guide employees through the communications gridlock.

'There's no physical maximum on the number of messages you can send or receive,' she said. 'But it's like building a six-lane motorway. Very soon the traffic will increase to fill it.'

© Telegraph Group Limited, London 1999

All in a day's work

The average middle-management executive sends or receives 178 messages or documents every day

Phone calls	56	Paper messages	9
E-mail messages	23	Mail (traditional post)	7
Voice-mail messages	21	Cellular phone calls	5
Faxes	15	Overnight courier deliveries	2
Post-it notes	14	Express mail delivery	1
Phone message slips	13	Local messenger delivery	1
Inter-office/Internal mail messages	11		

Source: Gallup/Institute for the Future/San Jose State University study of Fortune 1000 companies

Is this the end of nine to five?

The NatWest takes flexi-working to new lengths with plan for 1,826-hour year

Bank staff could lead the way in putting the final nail in the coffin of the traditional nine-to-five working week.

NatWest wants them to sign up for a flexi-year – of 1,826 hours.

And experts say that 'choose when you work' schemes are likely to become the norm in the 21st century with benefits for both sides. For staff it can mean making time for the family, leisure, or shopping during what has been the normal working week.

In theory, they could work around the clock for seven or eight months and take the rest of the year off although firms will want to ensure that their entire staff don't disappear in the summer.

For companies such as banks and retailers it means a minimum number are available to work 24 hours seven days a week – and there are also big savings by doing away with the expense of overtime.

It gives manufacturers the security of knowing they can call in staff to work long hours to get a big order out on time. More than 60 per cent of firms now operate some form of flexi-time, allowing employees to work when they choose within their normal week.

NatWest says its main aim is to ensure more staff are on duty at the busiest periods such as lunchtimes and Saturdays.

It has been piloting the scheme in a number of areas but now wants to introduce it for all its 15,000 employees.

However it first has to persuade the banking union Bifu, which is unhappy that members will lose overtime pay and extra cash for Saturday work, and is threatening industrial action unless its concerns are met. But Mark Hastings of the Institute of Management said the loss is 'a small price to pay for a better working system that is better suited to how we need to manage our lives into the next Millennium'.

He said it offered particular benefits to working couples with children. 'We know the stresses of

> '**People can juggle their hours to get out to the shops when it is less busy, to fit in with child care hours, and make sure they are at home when the plumber is due to call'**

trying to achieve a balance between work and home life are quite extraordinary,' he said. 'This is a response to that.'

He said flexible working originated as a way of cutting costs but now the big demand was coming from employees and customers who are becoming used to a 24-hour society, with shops open seven days a week and telephone banking.

Each system has to be tailored to the firm involved. Often it involves staff working fixed minimum hours each day to ensure that a certain number are on duty at any time.

A number of household companies, including BT, Eagle Star, First Direct bank, Burton, Asda and Sainsbury's, are operating similar schemes for at least some of their staff.

Angela Edward of the Institute of Personnel and Development said: 'People can juggle their hours to get out to the shops when it is less busy, to fit in with child care hours, and make sure they are at home when the plumber is due to call.

'There need to be rules, for example on the amount of notice given, warning staff they will be required to work extra hours.'

On overtime, she said: 'It need not be such a loss. Under this system you get a much more stable income. With overtime, pay can vary wildly.'

© The Daily Mail
May, 1998

Job insecurity leads to stress epidemic

By Seumas Milne

Stress at work is fast becoming an epidemic as the growing impact of long hours, increasing workloads, job insecurity and bullying has taken its toll over the last decade.

It is now recognised as the biggest occupational health problem, with a price tag of around £5 billion a year and up to 6 million working days lost, according to the Health Department.

With compensation claims now topping the list of cases brought against employers by trade unions, the Health and Safety Executive has issued guidelines and warned employers it intends to crack down on those who fail to tackle stress.

In a TUC survey of 8,000 health and safety union representatives, three out of four described stress as a major hazard, up from two-thirds two years ago. It was the most frequently cited problem in all organisations but the HSE says managerial, professional and clerical staff, care workers, nurses and teachers are particularly vulnerable.

Half a million workers are affected every year by stress, which can contribute to asthma, heart disease, arthritis, migraine, ulcers and diabetes, depression and other mental health problems.

Jenny Bacon, the HSE director general, concedes that stress has increased partly because of the rise of those forms of work hailed as the way of the future, such as part-time working, home working and multiple contract employment.

> **Half a million workers are affected every year by stress, which can contribute to asthma, heart disease, arthritis, migraine, ulcers, depression and other mental health problems**

The growth of team working, noisy open-plan offices and 'hot-desking' – where workers are moved from one work station to another to encourage flexibility – have also been blamed.

Cary Cooper, of the Manchester school of management at the university's institute of science and technology, estimates that between a third and a half of all stress-related sickness absence is accounted for by workplace bullying.

That in turn is linked to the 'downsizing' and job insecurity associated with the 1990s labour market, he believes, with overworked and stressed managers replacing bosses with personality defects as the main bullying culprits. 'Management are giving vent to their frustrations.'

Among the successful personal injury compensation claims brought by unions last year was the case of the widow of a North East Essex Mental Health NHS Trust employee who had been driven to suicide by stress at work.

The man had been subjected to a 'vindictive, oppressive, ruthless and macho style of management,' according to the public services union Unison. His widow received £25,000 in an out-of-court settlement.

*© The Guardian
January, 1999*

New workers

Young people are shedding notions of loyalty and security to gain marketable and transferable skills, writes Helen Wilkinson

In spring 1996 I spent four days in a woodland retreat several miles outside Toronto, Canada, with 30 of North America's brightest and best graduates.

For those four days we put aside the realities of our working lives – long hours, increasing job insecurity – and dared to imagine another future. We were all in our twenties and thirties and well educated, and had lived through a middle-class recession. We were all too aware that the old rules no longer applied, and we were that weekend to brainstorm on what might take their place.

In contrast to our parents' generation, we did not spend much time discussing job security. Instead we discussed employability. But most of the time we talked about wanting interesting and varied work: work which gave our lives meaning as well as bringing us a pay cheque at the end of the month.

We talked about wanting a working environment that gave us a sense of community, a mission, shared goals, as well as communal spaces for relaxation and sociability.

And we talked about re-organising the workplace so that it facilitated a better balance between work and home. We talked about the virtues of flexible working and about the importance of company benefits, such as sabbaticals and educational and parental leave.

But above all we dreamed about a future in which our working and personal lives were in sync rather than in tension. This sounds utopian, a far cry from the messy realities of today where conflicts between work and personal life define the culture.

Certainly the gap between our aspirations and reality could not be starker. Although we talked about wanting balance, the harsh facts are that those of us in work are working harder than ever.

The Families and Work Institute's recent study of America's changing workforce found that, contrary to popular mythology, our generation works harder and longer than our peers did a generation ago. In Britain it is the same story.

It is trends such as this that explain why balance has become the leitmotif of the new generation, and why even the childless and single say they want a better balance between work and personal life.

The old rewards system – a job for life with its security and stability in return for hard work and loyalty – no longer resonates for this generation. A large body of research shows that people born in the 1960s and 1970s are developing quite a distinct set of attitudes to work and its role in their lives – a work ethic distinct from the Protestant work ethic of the past, which saw work as morally redeeming.

The reasons are not hard to see. Young people today are at the cutting edge of the revolution in our workplaces. They expect to change jobs and learn new skills repeatedly. Their approach to work is more transactional. They trust less and rely on themselves more.

In place of old-style corporate loyalty, economic reality has taught them that they must keep their options open. Pension plans and

> **Young people have a different vision of how their security can be achieved**

steady career advancement have less attraction than what an employer can teach here and now. Fixed jobs have less appeal than project-based work which provides variety, builds expertise and increases marketable and transferable skills.

Young people have a different vision of how their security can be achieved. The key is employability, and security is increasingly seen to come from having the skills and confidence to move between jobs.

The Protestant work ethic, encouraging hard work, loyalty and commitment in return for economic security, is no longer in keeping with the spirit of the times. Balance is the buzzword. Synergy Brand Values, a corporate consultancy specialising in cultural change, dubs today's young the tao generation for their desire to achieve a healthy interdependence between their working lives and their personal lives.

One implication of this new work ethic is that young people today want their work to be measured in terms of results not 'face time' in the office. In this sense, the tao generation is stealing a march on its elders as it challenges the culture of 'presenteeism' that pervades much of corporate culture.

Many employers are ill at ease with this approach. Some ask why they should be committed to training or generous contracts if staff feel no loyalty. They want to be sure that it makes commercial sense to change working routines. But there are indications that change may be forced on them.

Many high fliers of this generation have opted out of mainstream corporate culture and have set up their own thriving businesses.

Organisations whose cultural and financial capital depends on their ability to recruit and retain to-morrow's business leaders are waking up to the fact that they must adapt or lose out.

Their own market research is telling them that the new generation distinguishes between winner and loser organisations.

Those that appeal demonstrate their modernity in a variety of ways: female and ethnic minority employees in senior posts, flexible working conditions, other company benefits and ease with new technologies.

Those that are losers remain dominated by middle-aged grey suits and are struggling with the Internet.

But if the benefits of the information age and the values and aspirations of tomorrow's workers are to be realised, there will need to be action on the part of governments as well as leading-edge employers.

For not all the young are well equipped for this brave new world of economic insecurity; not all can strike a hard bargain with employers.

The new work ethic can help only a quarter or a fifth of the population, those with higher education, to advance. Those leaving school with few or no qualifications cannot demand anything from employers, and the insecurity of the labour market is to them a threat, not an opportunity.

Their trust, as well as their potential, needs to be fostered if they too are to win through in the new millennium.

• Helen Wilkinson is a research associate at the New York-based Families and Work Institute and a member of the National Work/Life Forum sponsored by BT in the UK. She can be reached via email at hwilkinson@families andwork.org

© The Guardian
January, 1999

Speaking up, speaking out!

The 2020 Vision Programme. Information from the Industrial Society

Introduction

The 2020 Vision Programme was launched by the Industrial Society in Autumn 1995, primarily as a result of concern that young people's voices are rarely heard in important political, economic and social debates. Yet young people will, by the year 2020, be key decision-makers – as parents, managers, entrepreneurs, community leaders, employees and policy-makers.

Qualitative research

Our initial research showed clearly that young people are both aware of and concerned about major economic and social issues. Further qualitative research by MORI during 1996 recorded the views of young people all over the UK – from inner cities, small towns and rural areas. These group discussions and one-to-one interviews captured a range of views, values and aspirations.

Codes

These are the codes used throughout the text to refer to data from various surveys and research:
Q – MORI qualitative research (14 focus groups and 44 1:1 interviews, 159 young people)
S – MORI schools 'omnibus' survey (169 schools, 4,188 11-16-year-olds)
A – MORI adult 'omnibus' survey. (961 16-25-year-olds)
B – Industrial Society/State of Flux 'black box' survey. (3,624 12-25-year-olds)
I – Industrial Society focus groups

What work means to young people

Most people regard work as an extremely important part of people's lives. However, they are aware of how labour market conditions and other factors can limit opportunities.

Participants strongly disagree with the media image of 'workshy' young people who do not want to work, and 81% of 12-25-year-olds have had some kind of paid work experience (B). Yet some participants express reservations about young people starting work at too early an age, suggesting that it could affect their school work and give them a negative view of the world of work.

The importance of work

45% of 16-25-year-olds (A) say that work gives meaning to life, with one in ten strongly agreeing. Young men are more likely to believe that they must have a job in order to be a member of society (34% of 16-25-year-old men, compared with 26% of women in that age group: A).

The need to work

The majority of young people believe that people should work. Some participants take a hard line on those who are genuinely 'workshy', advocating the removal of state support or compulsory voluntary work on behalf of the community.

Others feel that if people are 'workshy' the problem is not lack of motivation to work, but lack of opportunities to use and develop their skills.

The positive aspects of work

Young people say that getting on with the people you work with makes a job enjoyable (73% of 11-16-year-olds: S; 67% of 16-25-year-olds: A).

50% of 16-25-year-olds in social classes A and B say that having lots of challenges makes a job enjoyable, compared with 38% of those in social classes D and E (A).

Over a quarter think that a job is more enjoyable if it benefits society or helps others (26% of 11-16-year-olds S; 28% of 16-25-year-olds: A). 78% of 11-16-year-olds (S) and 61% of 16-25 year-olds: (A) think that decent pay is an important thing to look for in a job.

The negative aspects of work

Lack of respect and lack of recognition within the workplace are viewed as the main negative aspects of work (Q). Other problems are working long hours, doing boring and monotonous work, being underemployed, being in low-paid, low-status jobs, and being in a career you don't enjoy.

Working with the public is generally seen as a negative factor in a job. Only 15% of 11-16-year-olds (S) and 24% of 16-25-year-olds (A) think dealing with the public would make a job enjoyable (although young people aged 16-25 from social classes D and E are more likely to see this as an enjoyable factor in work than those from social classes A and B (31% compared with 24% respectively: A)).

How young people define work

A general definition emerges of work as productive activity that does not necessarily have to be paid employment (Q). Young people feel it is important to have the opportunity to be acknowledged for their contribution, and they feel that a work role can give you social status and a sense of identity.

Hard work

'Hard work' is seen as employment which is challenging, demanding or stressful, or a combination of all three (Q). It is sometimes seen as work you have to do just to survive, or tiring responsibilities – such as being a mother.

Easy work

'Easy work' is defined as work which is enjoyable and stress-free (Q). It might involve having control over what you do, or getting paid for doing something you enjoy doing anyway.

Role models for work

It is clear that young people's most influential role models for working life are to be found within the family network (Q). However, working parents are not always viewed positively; while parents in professional occupations were generally admired by their children, parents in unskilled and semi-skilled manual jobs were often felt to be exploited and poorly rewarded. One of the main criticisms of parents' jobs is that they have to spend too much time at work rather than at home. Hard work is seen to limit time for relationships, and is thus perceived as a negative factor causing instability and insecurity.

Having a variety of working adults pursuing different careers within a family seems to broaden a young person's horizons yet, when faced with the stresses of today's insecure working environment, young people sometimes choose a 'safe' career rather than one they really prefer (Q).

In many cases (and especially when parents work in manual jobs) young people have aspirations to do something different from their parents. Some young people don't want to work as hard or to carry out low-status jobs for too little reward (Q).

They often emphasise (Q) the importance of and need for qualifications, not only to enter their ideal occupation but also to ensure that they don't have to do the same jobs as their parents.

Because some young people have nobody in employment in their immediate family, all they know about is the injustice and soul-destroying nature of unemployment. These young people often have few opinions (Q) about issues which affect the world of work – with the obvious exception of unemployment, which has often dominated their lives.

Work in the future

The majority of young people acknowledge that there are few 'jobs for life' any more. Although many have a sense of personal optimism and believe that they will go on to have a career, there is a degree of collective pessimism about a future which could be dominated by high unemployment and more automation (Q). Although some acknowledge the need for continuous learning there is little reference to career planning.

Indeed, young people often display a contradictory response towards trends in the world of work. For example, many young people we spoke to (Q) aspire to stable careers, and over half of 12-25-year-olds (53%: B) believe they will always be employed – in the same organisation (29%) or in consecutive jobs with different organisations (24%). Yet 28% believe that in ten years' time there will be fewer people working, and 40% think that there will be more automation at work with robots replacing people (B).

Over half of 12-25-year-olds (B) predict that in ten years' time there will be more people working at home (58%) and 34% think there will be more flexible working arrangements. 36% of young women (B) think there will be more childcare provided at work in ten years' time, although only 13% of young men agree.

Self-employment

Only 6% of 12-25-year-olds think that they are likely to work for themselves (B). Many participants express fears about the difficulties surrounding self-employment – most notably the lack of support, security, information and advice (Q). Young people are also worried about losing the social aspects of work even if they gained the freedom – through self-employment – of doing their 'own thing'. For some, the very idea of self-employment is 'family unfriendly' (Q).

Working time

37% of 11-16-year-olds (S) say that being in control of the hours you work would make a job enjoyable (24% of 16-year-olds compared with 48% of 11-year-olds). The response was even lower among 16-25-year-olds, where only 18% say they want a job where they can manage their own time (A).

Working conditions

56% of 11-16-year-olds (S) and 54% of 16-25-year-olds (A) feel that good working conditions are one of the most important aspects of a job.

Job security

Unsurprisingly, 16-25-year-olds show a significantly greater degree of interest in job security (53%: A) than 11-16-year-olds (38%: S), as the need to support themselves into the long-term becomes a reality.

Coping with unemployment

50% of 12-25-year-olds (B) say they would try and become better qualified if they became unemployed, and 35% said they would seek specialist training.

Young women are more likely

to have a proactive approach to their working futures, while young men tend to expect opportunities to come to them. More young men said that if they were unemployed they would be likely to wait for the right job to come along (29% of men compared with 21% of women: B), and more young women said they were likely to take careers advice (38% of women compared with 30% of men: B).

23% of 22-25-year-olds (B) indicate they would think about going abroad if they found themselves unemployed, compared with 16% of 12-15-year-olds. However, only 8% of young people (B) say they would move to another region, perhaps feeling that the same barriers to employment exist across the UK.

Trade unions and rights at work

Few young people know much about trade unions (Q), but those that do think unions have less power than they once had, and suspect fears about job security have rendered unions relatively ineffective at defending workers' rights. It may be that the decline in trade union representation has reinforced many young people's view that it's 'every employee for themselves'.

Pay structures

Young people feel strongly (Q) that current pay structures across different jobs and sectors are inappropriate. Some feel that those in top jobs

(especially in the privatised utilities) should be paid less than they currently receive. Others say that those in caring professions should be better paid, as they contribute more to society.

Not only do some young people disapprove of low pay and wide pay differentials (Q), but the majority (61% of 12-25-year-olds: B) believe that the government should raise money for better services by taxing high earners more.

Minimum wage

There is some support for the introduction of a minimum wage, to protect those at the bottom of the employment hierarchy. A few participants also suggest there should be a 'maximum wage', with the surplus wealth redistributed among the rest of the workforce (Q).

Priorities for work

For the majority of young people being happy in their work, especially getting on well with colleagues, is a very important aspect of a job. Many participants aspire to a balance between pay and happiness, with views influenced to some extent by age, gender and social class (Q).

Financial reward

Although young people see pay as the key factor in a job, salaries are less important to older participants than to younger ones (78% of 11-16-year-olds: S, compared with 61% of

16-25-year-olds: A) perhaps because younger participants – not yet in work – focus on material benefits, while older participants recognise the social and other benefits of work (Q).

The material aspect of work is more important to men than women. 73% of 16-25-year-old men say that the main reason they work is to earn money, compared with 58% of women in the same age group (A).

59% of young people aged 16-25 in social classes A and B say that the main reason they work is to earn money, compared with 71% of those in that age group in social class C2. Qualifications, as well as class, are a factor, as 73% of 16-25-year-olds with vocational qualifications, compared with 54% of those in that age group with degrees, say that financial reward is the main reason for working (A).

Being valued at work

49% of 12-25-year-olds stress the importance of being valued at work, a factor that increases with age (44% of 12-15-year-olds compared with 61% of 22-25-year-olds: B).

44% of 11-16-year-olds (S) believe that being appreciated by your manager or boss would make work enjoyable, yet this declines to 36% among 16-25-year-old (A).

Promotion and status

Unsurprisingly, promotion and job prospects become increasingly important with age (32% of 11-16-year-olds: S rising to 50% of 16-25-year-olds: A).

Yet young people do not seem to seek status at work in the way it has traditionally been important. Only 6% of 11-16-year-olds (S) and 5% of 16-25-year-olds (A) believe that status and an important position are key elements in a job.

Barriers to employment

Young people repeatedly highlight lack of experience and various forms of discrimination as barriers to employment (Q). Participants mention discrimination against people in marginalised situations (such as homeless young people), women, those from minority ethnic groups, people with disabilities, and gay and lesbian young people.

Some referred to the vicious circle regarding experience; that is, you can't get a job without experience, but you can't get experience without a job.

'Work is doing something beneficial, worthwhile towards society . . . and getting a reward for it.'

'I'd like to have a career . . . a job with prospects rather than having a job one week, then having to change and go to do something else next week.'

'I was earning more money where I was working before, but . . . I took this job because it meant that I got my life back and got time to spend with my fiancée.'

Key findings

Work

- 81% of 12-25-year-olds have had some experience of paid work.
- 61% of 16-25-year-olds said the most important thing they look for in a job is good pay; good working conditions are their second choice (54%)
- 67% of 16-25-year-olds said getting on well with colleagues made a job enjoyable.
- 53% of 12-25-year-olds believed they were likely to be in permanent employment with the same employer or consecutive employers; 40% said there would be increased automation, and 28% thought there would be higher unemployment.

'I was working full-time as a trainee . . . it was an awful job . . . the wages were awful, but I still went and did it.'

- The above is an extract from *Speaking Up, Speaking Out!* – The 2020 Vision Programme Summary Research Report, produced by the Industrial Society. See page 41 for address details.

© The Industrial Society

For love or money

Child labour explored. Angela Bolton, Phil Mizen and Chris Pole asked children why they work and where the money goes

Child employment is riding high on the current policy agenda. A cross-departmental review of legislation is examining what is often described as a hidden or invisible phenomenon. True, most children work illegally outside the permitted hours or in prohibited jobs. But why should it continue to be represented as a hidden issue, when most children have worked by the time they are 16 and such work is taken for granted in many British families? Perhaps it is because numerous surveys have failed to explore the context of children's work. Child workers' everyday experiences, family circumstances and motivations remain something of a mystery, their perspectives unexplored, their parents' views unknown.

To address the first of these gaps, we asked 70 young workers aged 12-16 in the Midlands, East Anglia and South Wales to keep a year-long record of their work in burger bars, cafes, pubs, farms and shops. Some early themes from the research have proved extremely revealing of family lives in Britain. Unsurprisingly, money is the major motivation to work, but over time a more complex story has emerged. Exploring this further we find that part-time wages fund one young person's 'extras' but another's 'basics'.

American studies tend to see early employment as indicative of disengagement from education or the pressure of youth's pursuit of inflated, leisured lifestyles and luxury goods. Whilst British society is increasingly consumerist, the spending reported to us hardly ranks as the pursuit of 'luxury' lifestyles. It is more a case of childhood and the costs of parenting being inflated by broad social change, an example being the increasing cost of privatised leisure and sports activities. It is these trends which arguably pressurise parents, and by proxy, children.

We have heard little in the way of 'conspicuous consumption'. Many children work to buy 'extras' rather than essentials, but these generally turn out to be mundane not luxury items: CD singles; make-up; bus and taxi fares; pet food; snacks during school; a weekly magazine. Some buy cigarettes and alcohol. Others save for larger items: a bike; a cheap CD player; things they believe parents cannot afford. Most buy clothes. Many barter with parents who barter in return – 'You buy this and I'll buy that'. Part-time work pays for sports, clubs or hobbies. It enables friends to meet in safe places and to participate in activities encouraged as part of the natural process of growing towards independence. For some, like Mark, the financial situation at home meant that starting work at 11 or 12 was the only route to these normative activities of the teenage years: '(Working) just brings a little bit of money for your pocket or it takes a bit of stress off your mom, so, anything you can find you gotta do.'

Others started work at 14 or 15 in search of a degree of independence but knowing that they had a parental safety net. Unlike those who worked to relieve pressure on parents, they would not go without if the work dried up or they chose to opt out. A

'My mother thought it would be good experience to know what it was like in the real world where you have to work for a living and money isn't handed out on a plate'

---

minority did spend money on essential items, suggesting they were no longer fully dependent. Kaitlin, 15, wanted her own money to allow her unemployed parents to concentrate on younger siblings: 'My mother . . . has got two other children which are younger than me, and she don't have a lot of money each week, so I would rather earn my own money instead of having to nag (her) for money when I know she hasn't got it.' A surprising proportion gave or lent money to tide parents over or buy food, and subsidised and entertained younger siblings from their own wages.

Child employment seems to shed light on a society where young people are dependent on parents for longer and longer periods whilst, simultaneously, more and more children experience family breakdown, leading to poverty or economic hardship. With a fifth of dependent children living in workless households, and many more in work-poor households where money is tight, we should not be surprised when in some families it is a case of 'all hands on deck' or when older children try to absorb some of their own costs. Perpetuating the notion

of hidden child labour can stigmatise families where children work in response to straitened financial circumstances. The inference is that child employment is hidden by a minority of uncaring parents, and is an aberration rather than a normal experience. Ignoring the economic context implies it is unimportant. However the accelerated costs associated with caring for older children may be problematic, not just in workless households, but also for working families who can struggle to stay abreast of an increasingly consumerist society.

The degree of family help in finding work suggests that the relationship between family economics and child employment may prove to be a valuable barometer of the pressure upon families in contemporary Britain. Most children relied on similar family, informal and word-of-mouth contacts to adults seeking work. Some reported active encouragement from parents: 'My mother thought it would be good experience to know what it was like in the real world where you have to work for a living and money isn't handed out on a plate' (Mary, 14). Ronan, 15, worked alongside his mum in a commercial kitchen (illegal for someone of his age). He reported that, ' . . . it was my mum that keeps urging me to get like, some money because she's always paying for my (sports) subs and everything . . . She goes, "Oh you need to get a job to help me a bit sometimes", when she's stuck for money.'

These emerging themes beg systematic exploration of the relationships between working children,

poverty and hardship, and the costs of child-rearing in the later years of childhood. If part-time work proves the only way for some children to participate in society, then this issue reflects upon the state of family fortunes and young people's citizenship in an increasingly consumerist society. As such it concerns us all.

All names of young people have been changed. The 'Work, Labour and Economic Life in Late Childhood' Project is based in the Department of Social Policy and Social Work, University of Warwick,

funded by the ESRC 'Children 5-16: Growing into the 21st Century' Programme and is a collaborative project with NCH – Action for Children.

Dr Phil Mizen, a lecturer in Social Policy at Warwick, and Dr Chris Pole, a lecturer in Sociology at the University of Leicester, are Project Directors. Angela Bolton is the project Research Fellow.

Savings
Nearly a third (32 per cent) of families did not have any savings in

1995/96. Lone parents with dependent children were the most likely to have no savings; almost three-quarters (73 per cent) of these families had no savings at all. Retired couples had the most savings, with almost a third (31 per cent) having £20,000 or more.

• The above is an extract from *Family Policy*, the bulletin of the Family Policy Studies Centre. See page 41 for address details.

© *Family Policy Studies Centre*
Autumn ,1998

Children 'not ready for work of tomorrow'

**By Barrie Clement,
Labour Editor**

Unless the education system undergoes immediate and revolutionary change 'millions' of Britons will be condemned to a life without work.

The Government and business are showing a 'worrying lack of understanding about the pace and extent of change', according to one of the country's foremost independent think-tanks.

In a sideswipe at the Chancellor of the Exchequer's tough economic policy, a hard-hitting critique published yesterday by the Royal Society of Arts said government must recognise the need to create employment as well as control inflation.

And instead of concentrating on cramming general knowledge into young people, schools should also impart practical 'competences' so that pupils can survive in the brave new work of flexibility.

The study declares that educational institutions are preparing people for a world which no longer exists.

Written by Valerie Bayliss, the report, *Redefining work*, says that incessant reforms of the Eighties and Nineties 'bolted change on to a system which is essentially 19th century'.

Ms Bayliss said young people wanted their education to prepare

them for the real world with skills they need to live and work.

To prepare for the new millennium the education system should be built around 'competences' such as literacy, numeracy, familiarity with information technology and an understanding of the concept of 'proof'. Young people should also be equipped to acquire knowledge and an ability to manage their time and finances.

Ms Bayliss argues that there has already been a revolutionary change in the world of work over the last two decades. Some 70 per cent of the new jobs created in the last five years have not been full-time or permanent. The era of the traditional,

---

The study declares that educational institutions are preparing people for a world which no longer exists

---

permanent job was quickly coming to an end and the pace of change was accelerating.

Workers, however, had a limited ability to deal with such flexibility, she believes. Around half of the adult population left school at 15 and half of those have had no formal education since.

While ministers had made a start in reforming the benefits system, it was essential that the unemployed should be encouraged to become more employable by constantly updating and changing their skills. She contended that after three months on the dole, a condition of benefit should be that the claimant improves his or her employability.

The report calls for a Learning Institute to encourage a lifelong process of education. The institute would provide the research on which to base the new system.

Many people distrusted the advice they received from financial companies. The financial sector needed to redesign their products to cope with the new uncertainties.

For environmental reasons the Government would eventually give tax concessions for teleworking, so that most people would work from home at least some of the time.

© *The Independent*
April, 1998

What do young people want from work?

By Janet Smithson and Suzan Lewis, Manchester Metropolitan University

This article is based on a trans-national study in five European countries (UK, Ireland, Portugal, Sweden and Norway) examining perceptions of work and family, among a wide range of young people aged 18-30. The young people in all the five countries value jobs which provide challenge, enjoyment, opportunities for development, social benefits and reasonable pay. Adequate pay is related to independence from parents. This is particularly important in Portugal where most of the young people living with their parents long to find a steady job and have their own place.

The notion of career is taking on new meanings. Women in all the countries are as likely as men to talk about a career or what the British group of secretarial students call a 'career job', that is one with prospects. But a career is increasingly defined as a series of jobs with different employers rather than a continuous career with one employer. Women are still more likely than men to anticipate a career break or a break from full-time work when they have children, although some of the men in all five countries say they would like to do so.

Flexibility

Flexible working arrangements and opportunities to lead a balanced life are highly important to this generation. However, there is also a view that flexibility must be for everyone – men and women, parents and non-parents. If parents are perceived to be given special treatment, or if it is colleagues that have to make concessions for working parents, this can create resentment. Some of the British and Irish participants resent what they perceive as preferential treatment of parents. They want recognition of other non-work responsibilities. At the same time many feel that single working mothers should be supported.

A psychological contract

It appears that a new form of psychological contract – the un-written mutual understanding between employers and employees – is emerging. This is one in which employees want opportunities to develop their skills and abilities, to be treated equitably and as whole people, to work flexibly and to achieve a work-life balance. In return they too expect to be flexible and committed to their organisations while they are employed.

This age group is particularly affected by the trend towards fixed-term and temporary contracts in all the countries studied. Young people are realistic about the labour market, and there is no expectation of jobs for life, but they do want some security in the long-term. These young adults are adapting their actions and expectations in various ways. However, they are often very concerned about the longer-term implications. The participants make a distinction between short term insecurity, which is generally viewed

as 'acceptable', especially at a stage when they are gaining skills and experience in the job market, and long-term insecurity, which is seen as problematic, especially when combined with taking on other adult roles such as house buying, or starting a family. Although many young adults choose to postpone having children and settling down, there is a definite sense of the 'biological clock' limiting time for having children for the women in the groups (and also for some of the men).

Social benefits

One issue of particular concern is the importance of permanent contracts for entitlement to parental leave and other rights. In Sweden, where there are more rights for contract and temporary workers, the women still feel that they will not be able to claim many benefits in practice. In Portugal, many young people are hired as independent workers (on 'green receipts') which does not give them access to social benefits such as unemployment benefits when out of work, and they feel especially insecure and reliant on family for support.

The changing labour market, and in particular the increase in insecure work, whether perceived or actual, creates tensions when young adults try and plan for the future. Many of this age group are still in a precarious work situation, and can reasonably expect to still be in precarious work for at least a few more years. This is a major concern for many of them.

The study will be published by Midland Bank as a report called *Futures on Hold* in September. Contact the Work Life Research Centre for details: 0161 247 2546 or 2556.

© New Ways to Work Newsletter November, 1998

Juggling: it's not the way to relax

So much to do, so little time. Ann Treneman finds that life is hard for working families

Hannah Marie Dent knew that something had to change when, during her afternoon shift at the Golden Wonder factory in Scunthorpe, she forgot to put the salt in the crisps. Her mind was elsewhere – worrying about whether her three children were home from school. 'I got into trouble for that and I thought, this just isn't on,' she says. Her solution was to switch to the night shift and, despite all the exhaustion and scheduling complications, she is convinced it was the right thing.

'I really do like this much better. I can get my housework done. I've got more time for the kids. I can read with them and do their spelling and homework. And we can go to open evenings and school plays,' she says.

It also means that she and her husband, Shaun, run what is almost a round-the-clock shift system. They figure that, all in all, they have about half an hour together during the day. 'It doesn't do much for your sex life,' says Shaun. Hannah Marie says she's not too bothered about that.

Tomorrow night, the BBC's *Having It All* season ends with a programme called *Juggling* (the Dents are one of three couples who star in it). At first I thought there was some mistake with the title. Even the word is a blast from the past. It belongs to the Eighties era of power shoulders and Dallas reruns. Those were the days when people aspired to juggle, and women's magazines carried articles about how to do more in less time.

She magazine was 'for women who juggle their lives'. Then its editor, Linda Kelsey, left her job after finding the juggling too stressful, and the magazine's motto changed. People started to talk about simplify-

ing their lives and the women's glossies to fill up with articles on yoga.

But in the real world, our lives in the Nineties have become more, not less, complicated. Employment trends show that we are working longer hours and have much less job security. Time is the most valuable commodity for many families.

Stress expert Cary Cooper says: 'It is the relationship between the husband and wife that troubles me. Is it a coincidence that we have the longest working hours and the highest divorce rate in Europe?'

Two out of three families now have two incomes. Most women with young children work, both out of choice and necessity. For instance, Hannah Marie supported Shaun through years of study to become a health and safety expert and still provides the family's main income while the business finds its feet. The Dents may seem extreme in some ways, but their circumstances are not unusual.

W. Stokes-Jones, editor of *Planning for Social Change*, said: 'Juggling didn't go away. It just became the norm. It is now par for the course. That's the way with

trends. You can tell when they really take hold – they become invisible.' And lucrative. He notes that the three fastest-growing retail markets are takeaway food, domestic help and childcare. All are the tools of the jugglers.

Shaun Dent, at 37, tries to cheat time in many ways. He keeps his car clock set 15 minutes ahead. He asks me if I'd like a tea or, even better, a quick tea (evidently this is the powdered kind). When I ask him about juggling, he just looks exasperated. 'I think it's past juggling. It's just what we do.' Hannah Marie nods. 'It's like normal life now.'

Just listening to their schedule is exhausting. Hannah Marie's day ends at 6am, just as her husband's begins. They meet in the kitchen, where one or the other is making up the packed lunches for their three boys, aged between eight and 13. She goes to bed then and Shaun gets the children up and takes them to school before going to work.

Hannah gets up about 1pm and does the housework and some accounts for Shaun, before picking the children up from school and cooking their tea. When Shaun gets home, at about 7pm, he makes dinner for the two of them. She reads with the kids and, at 9pm, starts to get ready for work. Hannah figures she has almost no free time. 'But I do always watch *Coronation Street*,' she says.

Clare Paterson, who created the *Having It All* series, says that the whole thing started because she was so interested in juggling. 'It's the messy bits in our lives that are the most interesting. It's the school run and the pick-up. It's not the meal but the food preparation that is interesting,' she says.

She and her husband have three children. 'Even at the weekends there is a constant negotiation over who is going to do what,' she says. 'My husband will say, "What are the plans for the day?" The only real plan is to somehow get through it! And I just really wondered how other families coped with that.'

The film features three families of five. Anna and David are both lawyers and live in a lovely big house in Kent. Jody is a final-year student barrister and is married to Tom, a prison officer. And then there are the Dents in Scunthorpe. 'I was interested in looking at the similarities and differences,' says director Peter Gordon. 'But the similarities far outweigh any differences and they always are around the key issue. They are always asking: Are we doing the right thing by the children? There is a lot of guilt.'

Nor does money change things that much. Anna and David, for instance, can afford any amount of help, but often their only real chance to talk mid-week is during a shared car journey. 'When you compare Anna and David and Hannah and Shaun – even though there are probably hundreds of thousands of pounds' worth of difference in their earnings – what they are actually saying and feeling is very similar,' says Peter Gordon.

He adds that it seems to be generally agreed that it is the woman who makes the main concessions and that work, for everyone, was an area of calm compared to the chaos at home.

Novelist Maeve Haran ushered in the superwoman backlash a few years ago with her best-selling novel *Having It All*, in which her heroine trades in a high-powered job to spend more time with her children and less time writing lists. In some ways the book mirrored her life but, with three children and a full-time writing career, she still knows a lot about juggling. 'Oh, God yes, I'm just writing a list now as a matter of fact. If I didn't juggle, I wouldn't survive,' she says when I ring. 'But in one generation we've become much more child-centred as well as more career-oriented, so it's no wonder we all make so many lists.'

Shaun and Hannah Marie say that our interview is the longest time they've spent together for ages. I ask about the future. Shaun says when his business becomes more successful then he might be able to come home earlier. Hannah says she'll never give up work. 'It's my independence and I've always said my kids wouldn't go without.'

© The Independent
March, 1998

No question of multiple choice

Judith Green and Jonathan Upton on the increase in women whose work is never done

Multiple job-holding is not a new phenomenon. It has always been one of the ways in which women, in particular, juggle the competing demands of raising an income and raising a family. What is new, though, is the rapid growth of multiple job-holding and the reliance now placed upon it by many families.

Our research among almost 200 local authority workers in the north-east suggests that two in three either have or have had two or more jobs at the same time. And official statistics indicate that almost 1.3 million people hold more than one job, with evidence suggesting this may be a significant underestimate.

The expansion has occurred against a background of dramatic rises in part-time working, as well as a growth in temporary work and casualisation. In the north, where traditional heavy industries have been all but wiped out, about a third of all jobs are now part-time.

Our study focused on manual jobs where part-time working is the prevailing pattern. Working with the local branch of Unison, the public services union which commissioned the study, researchers from Northumbria university conducted a series of interviews and focus groups with school meals staff, cleaners, home care workers and school crossing wardens.

As many as two in three of the workers, most of whom were women, turned out either to be multiple job-holders or to have held more than one job in the past.

Unsurprisingly, financial pressure was the overwhelming reason for doing so. The benefits system, which is supposed to offer a safety net for the lower-paid, appeared to be ill-understood and seen as over-complicated – leaving some of those most in need excluded from help. Not least, it was evident that the system has difficulty coping with those who garner their income from a range of sources.

What was striking about the research were the difficult, arduous working situations that people were prepared to accept. Women would work three or four shifts in a single day, or come off a long night-shift and almost immediately go out to work again for another stretch of several hours' hard manual work. Two stories are typical:

- Lilian currently holds four different jobs. She is a part-time school cleaner, on a permanent contract for 15 hours a week; she works as a care attendant in a private residential home, which involves two overnight sessions a week; she does home care work for a private care agency, working a regular two afternoons a week; and she works as a cleaner in a private home on another two afternoons a week. Her usual working week amounts to 52 hours.
- Ada works as a home carer for the council; she works 27-30 hours in a typical week, with a block of work each morning, seven days a

week. She also works as a home carer for a voluntary organisation. In this case, she is in a 'pool' and has neither guaranteed hours, nor a permanent contract. She can be asked to work at very short notice and the hours are highly variable, ranging from none to as many as 28 a week. Ada's total working hours, therefore, vary from 30 to 60 a week.

Many of these part-time jobs were found to carry no sick pay or holiday entitlements and no pension schemes, meaning that workers were disadvantaged in illness, leisure and old age, as well as in their low pay.

For many working people, multiple job-holding is the only realistic strategy available, and it is no longer possible to dismiss the trend as a marginal issue. Policy-makers need to consider that many of the improvements in women's employment rights appear peripheral to the experience of lower-paid women workers; that trade unions look ill-equipped to meet the needs of workers who obtain their income from a number of different employers; and that many multiple job-holders may find the traditional emphasis on annual wage bargaining to be of much less practical benefit than measures such as subsidised child care and transport.

Above all, the Government needs to take full account of the extent of multiple job-holding in development of its promised minimum wage and the welfare-to-work programme. What is clear from the research is that a simplistic focus on numbers of jobs created often obscures important issues about not only the quality of work, but also the real impact on unemployment and well-being.

• Judith Green is a research fellow at the social welfare research unit of Northumbria university; Jonathan Upton is a Unison regional officer, currently on secondment to the Labour Party.

Women in their prime as main breadwinners

Revolution in earning power switches traditional roles. By Julia Timms

Women over 35 are the new financial force to be reckoned with as they reap the rewards of an amazing transformation in earning power.

Forty per cent of those in this age group are now the chief breadwinners in their households, compared with one per cent just ten years ago.

They are the fastest-growing section of the population in Britain and between them generate a total personal income of £99 billion a year.

Actresses such as Helen Mirren, Joanna Lumley, Cher and Goldie Hawn have shown that middle-aged woman need not fade into the background even when they are 'past their sell-by date'. All have enjoyed success in a youth-dominated industry and have immense professional clout.

Women in the workplace have also surged ahead with the likes of superwoman Nicola Horlick combining a top job with being a mother of five children.

And with that success has come independence. Fifty-six per cent of women questioned for a new survey said that they no longer needed a man for financial security.

More than half own a car and 62 per cent work either full or part time. A total of 1,000 women aged between 35 and 55 were questioned in face-to-face interviews. Of these, 67 per cent believe that women are no longer just the fairer sex but also the stronger sex. Their growing financial power and increased confidence has made them a lucrative target for advertisers.

The results of the survey, carried out by the IPC magazines group, will be used as part of a major sales offensive to tap into this sector.

Chantal Burns, advertising manager with IPC magazines, said: 'This important piece of research provides a clear insight into the fastest-growing highly-lucrative sector of the population. The role of the woman in society has changed so much over the last ten to 20 years, and the 40-year-old is nothing like she was then in terms of how she looks, feels or behaves.

'Women have become ageless in many respects, therefore companies need to evolve their thinking and really appreciate this market for what it is.

'At 40, some women will be starting a family and settling down, have been married for 20 years with kids who are leaving home or they could be single, at the peak of their careers or going back to work.'

Fitness guru Rosemary Conley, 51, said women's attitudes had changed enormously in recent years. She said: 'I'm not surprised by the results of this survey.

'I think that women have broken through the barrier of sex being an issue and that people have realised that women have a real contribution to make to society.

'We have become much more confident than we were ten years ago. Then we were looked upon as being either a housewife or a secretary.

'Now we have such great role models who are achieving great successes in their field. We also see far more glamorous older women around, which is fantastic.'

New employers

Jayne Buxton on why Asda is being clever as well as kind in enabling a cashier to both work her hours and attend her son's school concert

Family-friendly working practices; work-life balance; to a hard-driving business manager, these terms conjure up thoughts of disruption and cost. But need employers be afraid? Do family-friendly working practices – more popularly known as work-life balance initiatives – represent a net cost to business?

The evidence is that work-life balance is as good for business as it is for people.

Companies are already having to adapt: globalisation, which brings customers in disparate time zones, and advancing technology, responding to and creating new customer needs, are driving change.

Smart businesses, like Granada's television service division, use these forces to create new work options. At Granada, customer demand for service outside conventional working hours led to engineers being put on flexible contracts. Working more from home, managing their schedules, and benefiting from new technological support, engineers can manage their time so as to better meet customer needs while benefiting themselves from more flexible schedules and less commuting time. In the process, Granada's customer service gained on the competition.

Another aspect of the new business reality is that women are half the workforce, and two-thirds in some sectors such as health, hotels and teaching. A smart company supports women so they can give their maximum to the organisation.

If a shift-swap scheme at Asda, the supermarket chain, enables a cashier to work her weekly hours and attend her son's school concert, then it is clever as well as kind. The Midland Bank raised its retention rate for women on maternity leave from 30 to 80 per cent by allowing them to work flexibly on their return.

Retention of people, skills and knowledge is a strategic challenge for organisations. Companies are waking up to the effect of employee retention on customer retention and profitability. A study of Fortune 500 companies in the United States by Massachusetts Institute of Technology showed a link between employee loyalty and company productivity. The Gemini Consulting study found that two out of three workers would leave their jobs immediately to obtain either a small pay increase, more opportunity, or greater flexibility. Measures to improve work-life balance and flexibility are integral to increasing employee loyalty.

Women are half the workforce, and two-thirds in some sectors such as health, hotels and teaching

---

Work-life measures can also reduce the corporate health bill. Barclays Bank discovered that its job-sharing teams in one call centre had zero per cent sickness absence rates, as compared to 4.5 per cent for full-time employees. And the Families and Work Institute in New York found that employees who had more control over their working schedules were more likely to stay with the company, take initiative, and give their all toward achieving company objectives.

Human capital plays a growing role in corporate success and wealth: the US-based Brookings Institution says two-thirds of stock market value now lies in 'soft' attributes such as patents, processes, and customer and employee satisfaction.

Of course, the challenges of life-friendly working practices are not to be ignored. Not least is the fact that most managers are focused on the short term, while many of the benefits accrue in the long term. But for those brave enough the benefits are waiting to be enjoyed.

Pat Nazemetz is a champion of work-life efforts at Xerox. She insists: 'if you keep doing this stuff, you will get better business results'.

Xerox's chief executive, Paul Allaire, supports her, asserting that the family-friendly culture is a way of unleashing the creativity of Xerox employees.

Given the firm's record of productivity improvements of up to 30 per cent in some areas where it has conducted work-life experiments, business leaders could do far worse than follow the Xerox example.

-A REMINDER THAT YOU STILL HAVE A FAMILY-

• Jayne Buxton is author of *Ending the Mother War, Starting the Workplace Revolution*, Macmillan, £14.99.

© *The Guardian*
January, 1999

Plight of the have-it-alls who miss family life

By Briony Warden

Employees are sinking under the strain of juggling work and family life, researchers have found.

More than half feel they are missing seeing their children grow up and many regret the sacrifices they have to make for their jobs.

Almost half said pressure at work left them barely able to meet their commitments and responsibilities at home.

The struggle to have it all seems to have left parents and workers dissatisfied on all fronts, according to the biggest survey of Britain's work culture.

And the pressure shows no sign of easing. According to the survey, two-thirds of managers said they were expected to demand more and more from their staff.

Women were struggling most with the balance of work and home. Two out of three felt they had less time for their personal lives.

One in ten said they had delayed having children or sacrificed the chance to be a mother because of their careers.

But despite the increasing demands of the workplace, women appear to be getting more out of their jobs. More women than men said they gained most of their satisfaction in life from pursuing a career.

The survey found that work could also provide some relief when life at home became too complicated. One in three employees said there were times they would rather escape to work than cope with a sick parent or crying child at home. Overall, though, there is a strong commitment – in principle – to family life.

Four out of five people felt that home should always come first. But only four in ten felt they had got the balance right.

The survey found the 'having it all' culture of the Eighties has left workers in the Nineties torn by conflicting pressures at home and work.

'My husband and I are forced to work long hours, can't move, pay a fortune for childcare and have a miserable quality of life,' one woman in her 30s said.

'We have no time for the children, who will presumably suffer long term. No wonder none of our friends have them.'

More than half of the 5,500 men and women interviewed by consultants Ceridian Performance Partners and business magazine *Management Today* said they regretted sacrificing family life for the sake of their careers.

Many had missed school events or even parents' funerals. Others had not been home when a partner was seriously ill.

According to the survey, the biggest culprit was the British culture of working long hours.

Putting in fewer hours was top of the workers' wish list for a better quality of life.

Managers agreed. Two-thirds felt working long hours was confused with commitment and four in ten cited heavy workloads as a prime cause of staff turnover.

Ceridian Performance Partners' chief executive Liz Bargh said the sacrifices some people made for their jobs was 'shocking'. 'The report sends a clear signal – our present way of working is unsustainable,' she said.

'Business will be forced to work with their employees to balance work and life for compassion and competitiveness.'

© *The Daily Mail*
June, 1998

Full-time average hours usually worked* in the EU, 1996

Country		Males	Females	Country		Males	Females
Austria		40.2	39.8	Italy		39.8	36.4
Belgium		38.8	37.1	Luxembourg		40.4	37.7
Denmark		39.4	37.6	Netherlands		39.5	39.0
Finland		39.4	38.0	Portugal		42.7	39.3
France		40.5	38.8	Spain		41.0	39.6
Germany		40.4	39.3	Sweden		40.1	39.9
Greece		41.4	38.9	UK		45.8	40.6
Irish Republic		42.0	38.0	EU Average		41.3	39.0

* Employees only. Excludes meal breaks but includes regularly paid and unpaid overtime.

Source: Social Trends 1998

A helping hand for women 'returners'

Going to work after years at home takes confidence, and new skills. Sarah Jewell gets networking

Many women who take a career break to have children find when they want to get back to work that they have lost their self-confidence. They feel out of touch with the job market, and have not kept up with the latest computer technology.

Ann Gabriel, who took the 'Professional Updating' course at the University of Westminster, is now working for the Industrial Society. She spent 15 years bringing up her children but before they were born she worked as an industrial journalist, and wanted to do a course to get back up to date. Initially she thought she would do 'a little admin job', but then decided to go back into her chosen field. With support, her expectations rose: 'Without the course I wouldn't have had the confidence to approach the Industrial Society. I think there were bits of me that were dormant that suddenly came alive again; the course bridged the gap between home and work and made the transition as painless as possible.'

The Women Returners' Network was set up in 1984 by lecturers in higher education who recognised that women returning to work needed information, guidance, and often retraining.

Liz Bavidge, the director, understands how difficult it can be for a woman to get back to work after having children. She herself is a 'returner' who left her job as an executive of an oil company in London and moved to Halifax, where after a period as a housewife and mother she found it very hard to re-establish herself:

'I understand women who say that everything is passing them by, and their horizons have shrunk, because I was in that situation myself,' she says.

The WRN gets several hundred calls a month from women who need help and advice, and Liz Bavidge finds that 'often it gives them a real boost to discover that they are not the only one in this situation, and they are just delighted to talk to someone who understands'. The WRN has a comprehensive information database on sources of help with training, education and finding a job, and its national directory, 'Returning to Work', offers up-to-date details of courses.

One of the courses devised by the WRN, 'Professional Updating for Women', is aimed at women with a degree who are trying to get back into their chosen field of work. The course is free, and is currently taught in 10 universities around the country. Diana Wolfin, course co-ordinator at the University of Westminster, is enthusiastic about what it has to offer: 'I have to say it is brilliant. We care very much about all the women on the course and follow their progress carefully, even after they have left. We aim to help them regain confidence, and learn new skills that may have evolved since they left work.'

The course teaches IT skills such as word processing and making spread-sheets, which, as Diana Wolfin says, 'are some of the things which women who've been at home lack most of all'.

It also concentrates on image presentation and interview techniques, and includes a two-week work placement in a relevant area of employment. 'The networking aspect of the course cannot be underestimated,' she says. 'It is so important to share feelings about lack of confidence. Even women who've been in senior positions lose confidence after six months at home.' Most women do go on to get jobs, and for Diana Wolfin 'it is the greatest joy to see a woman come on the course feeling that she has got nothing to offer, and then leave with a job'.

• Women Returners' Network, 100 Park Village East, London NW1 3SE (0171-468 2290).

© The Independent
May, 1998

Maternity rights

Employers have certain legal obligations towards pregnant employees. This article gives the details

What special rights do pregnant employees have?

It is unlawful to dismiss a pregnent employee (or single her out for redundancy) for reasons connected with her pregnancy or maternity.

In addition, every pregnant employee who has given her employer proper notification of her pregnancy is entitled to:

- reasonable time off with pay for antenatal care (which may include relaxation and parent-craft classes)

- 14 weeks' maternity leave

- all her normal terms and conditions except wages or salary while she is on maternity leave

- suspension from work on full pay if there is an unavoidable health or safety risk to her as a new or expectant mother and suitable alternative work cannot be found.

In addition, pregnant employees who have completed two years' service or more with their employer, by the beginning of the 11th week before the week the baby is due, are entitled to an additional period of maternity absence.

Many pregnant women will also be entitled to Statutory Maternity Pay (SMP).

Employers should also bear in mind that detrimental treatment of an employee in connection with maternity may be unlawful sex discrimination.

When does maternity leave start and finish?

A pregnant employee can normally start her maternity leave at any time she chooses after the beginning of the 11th week before the week the baby is due – provided that she gives at least three weeks' notice, where reasonably practicable. The leave period continues for 14 weeks after it has started.

What if the baby is born before the date maternity leave was due to start?

The leave starts automatically on the date the baby is born.

What if a pregnant employee is absent from work because of illness?

A pregnant employee who is absent from work because of illness can normally take sick leave under the employer's usual arrangements. However, if the illness is related to her pregnancy and the absence occurs during the six weeks before the week the baby is due, her maternity leave starts automatically at that point.

Is the employee entitled to go back to her old job when she returns from maternity leave?

Yes. She is entitled to resume her normal job on the same terms and conditions as if she had not been absent. If a redundancy situation arises during her maternity leave, she must be offered any suitable alternative work that is available at that point.

When does the additional maternity absence start and finish?

The additional maternity absence (for which a woman with two years' service or more qualifies) starts at the end of the maternity leave period and continues up to the end of the 28th week after the week the baby is actually born. If the woman starts her maternity leave 11 weeks before the week the baby is due, she can therefore be absent for up to around 40 weeks in total.

A woman who qualifies for and intends to take advantage of the right to the additional maternity absence must inform her employer of this when giving notification of her pregnancy. She must also give her employer at least three weeks' notice of the date she intends to return from the additional absence, where reasonably practicable.

Is the employee entitled to go back to her old job when she returns from the maternity absence?

Normally. If, however, a redundancy situation has arisen during the additional absence period, or if there is some other genuine reason why her original job is no longer available, she must be offered any suitable alternative work that is available at the point when she wants to return.

In addition, an employer with five or fewer employees is under no obligation to take back a woman after the additional absence period if to do so would not be reasonably practicable. (In the event of a dispute, it would be for an Industrial Tribunal to decide what was reasonably practicable.)

What is the difference between maternity leave and maternity absence?

During maternity leave a woman is entitled to all her normal terms and conditions (continued accrual of holiday, for example, if it would normally accrue while she was at work) except wages or salary. During maternity absence, however, contractual matters such as this are for negotiation and agreement between the employer and employee (or their representatives).

What if a woman has more favourable maternity entitlements under her employment contract than under the law?

She can take advantage of whichever is more favourable in any particular respect.

What is Statutory Maternity Pay (SMP)?

SMP is payable by an employer for up to 18 weeks to women who:
- have 26 weeks' service or more by the end of the 15th week before the week the baby is due; and
- earn at least £64 per week.

Employers whose total gross National Insurance liability is £20,000 or less are reimbursed in full by the Government, with an additional 7% to cover the administrative costs of operating the scheme. Other employers are reimbursed at the rate of 92% of the SMP they pay out.

The rate of SMP is 90% of the woman's normal salary for the first six weeks and £57.70 per week for the remaining weeks.

Woman can get SMP only for weeks when they do not work.

Woman who do not meet the qualifying conditions for SMP may be entitled to claim Maternity Allowance (MA) direct from the Benefits Agency.

In what circumstances does suspension from work on full pay arise?

Employers must take account of the health and safety of new and expectant mothers and their babies. When assessing risks in the workplace they must take all reasonably practicable preventative steps to remove or control hazards. If a risk remains, the employer must offer the woman any suitable alternative work that is available, under no less favourable terms and conditions. If no such work is available, the employer must suspend the employee on full pay for as long as necessary to protect her health and safety.

What if an employer fails to meet legal obligations towards a pregnant employee?

An employee who considers that she has been denied her rights may complain to an Industrial Tribunal – or to the civil courts if the complaint is about a contractual matter. Complaints to an Industrial Tribunal should normally have to be made within three months of the date of the alleged infringement of rights.

Where can I get further information?

The following free publication, available from any Employment Service Jobcentre or direct from the DTI Publications Orderline on 0870 1502 500 may also be a useful source of information:
- *Maternity Rights* URN 96/909.

The Health and Safety Executive booklet *New and Expectant Mothers at Work* offers detailed guidance on assessing health and safety risks. It is a priced publication available from HMSO bookshops or from 0171 873 9090 (fax orders on 0171 873 8200).

The Advisory, Conciliation and Arbitration Service (ACAS) provides information and guidance on a wide range of employment and industrial matters. The service is free, confidential and impartial. ACAS's telephone number is in the telephone directory. *Employing People – a handbook for small firms* (price £3.00) and free leaflets about ACAS services are available from ACAS Reader Ltd on 01455 852225.

ACAS can conciliate in actual or potential complaints to Industrial Tribunals. Conciliation is free, voluntary, and attempts, through discussion, to help the parties to a dispute reach their own agreement.

- This information is one of a series of employment rights factsheets produced for small employers on behalf of the Department of Trade and Industry (DTI).

© Crown Copyright
April, 1998

Main types of statutory maternity and paternity provision in the EU

Country	Maternity leave	Maternity payment	Paternity leave
Austria	16 weeks	100% of earnings	None
Belgium	15 weeks	82% of earnings for the first month and 75% of earnings for remainder	3 days at 100% earnings
Denmark	18 weeks	Flat-rate equivalent to unemployment benefit	10 days flat-rate
Finland	17.5 weeks	Between 66% and 45% of earnings	6-12 days at birth, at same rate as maternity pay
France	16 to 26 weeks	84% of earnings	3 days
Germany	14 weeks	100% of earnings	None
Greece	14 weeks	100% of earnings	None
Ireland	14 weeks plus 4 weeks optional	70% of earnings, no payments for optional 4 weeks	None
Italy	5 months (20 weeks)	80% of earnings	None
Luxembourg	16 weeks	100% of earnings	None
Netherlands	16 weeks	100% of earnings	None
Portugal	90 days (13 weeks)	100% of earnings	None
Spain	16 weeks	75% of earnings	2 days 100% of earnings
Sweden	12 weeks	90% of earnings	2 weeks 80% of earnings
UK	40 weeks	90% of earnings for six weeks, flat rate for 12 weeks, remainder unpaid	None

Source: Ruxton, S. (1996). Children in Europe, London: NCH Action For Children

Parents at work

Flexible working

A flexible working pattern can be the ideal solution to balancing the responsibilities of family and working life more effectively. It can give you time to care for your child while allowing you to concentrate on your job fully when you're at work. It can, if managed correctly, be a lifesaver for you, and make economic sense to your employer.

An increasing number of employers are now introducing a range of family-friendly policies that allow their employees to achieve this balance and enhance the quality of their lives and those of their families. Flexible working practices to look out for, or ask your employer about include:

Part-time working: anything below the standard working week. It might mean you can leave early enough to pick the children up from school. But watch out for the boss who wants you to cram a full-time job into part-time hours or pay!

Flexi-time: where you can vary your hours but have a fixed core time and can take banked hours as flexi leave.

Job-sharing: where a job is split between two individuals.

Term-time working: allows you to be in a permanent full or part-time job while taking unpaid leave during agreed school holidays. Your pay may be averaged out over the year.

School hours working: where you work during school hours only (lets you drop the kids off and pick them up).

Compressed hours: where you work more hours each day, but fewer days of the week.

V-time (voluntary reduction in hours): born in the USA but now in the UK, V-time allows you to reduce your time at work by an agreed period.

When considering some form of flexible working it is worth spending some time in researching which type of flexible working would suit you best and to make sure that you put a good case to your employer.

Working from home: where you can work from home all or part of the week. Research suggests that professional and clerical jobs are the most suitable for home working. Whilst it can be done with older children, don't expect to be able to work and look after a baby at the same time.

Things to consider when researching flexible working:

- What kind of flexible working would best suit your needs
- What type of flexible working would best suit the demands of your job
- What would be the cost in terms of money, employment rights, pension, holidays, etc.
- How will this affect your employer – costs and savings, flexibility, manpower, management time
- Other examples of flexible working in your company
- What is your company's policy on flexible working, and what examples are there of flexible working in your company? (Your personnel department should be able to provide these details)
- What will the long-term implications be – will you, for example, be able to go back to full-time working later?

How to approach your employer

If you are a member of a trade union, speak to the local organiser before approaching your employer. When approaching your employer it is important to have a well-prepared proposal presented in person and on paper. Set out what flexible working patterns you want, how that will fit in with your job and try to emphasise the benefits to the organisation of the flexible option you have chosen. These might include:

- Retention of experienced employees who need to alter their hours
- Reduce the costs of recruitment and training of new staff
- Attract a more diverse range of candidates because of a flexible working package
- Greater commitment from employees
- Enable employees to have greater control of their own time so they can fit personal commitments around work hours more effectively

Think about how long you want the arrangements to last for. Is it short-term or permanent? If it is long-term you, and your employer, will probably want a review period to see how the new arrangements are going. Planning this may help allay anxieties.

For further information

New Ways to Work, 309 Upper Street, London, N1 2TY. Tel: 0171 226 4026. Provides information to individuals, employers and unions on a range of flexible working patterns.

The Employee's Guide to Flexible Working provides practical advice on preparing a flexible working proposal and how to approach your manager. £3.99 (£3.50 to members) inc p&p.

Family Friendly Pack: Flexible Working a practical guide for busy employers it provides a step-by-step guide to choosing and implementing the right policies for their organisation. £19.50 (£15.50 to members) inc p&p.

Both available from Parents at Work. See page 41 for address details.

© *Parents at Work*

What future for the female boss?

By Barrie Clement,
Labour Editor

Office workers are marching towards a bright, relaxing, hi-tech future encumbered by stone-age views on female bosses, especially among women themselves.

While workplaces will become like flexible, informal 'clubs', the overwhelming majority of women – and to a lesser extent their male colleagues – fervently hope they will be presided over by men.

Despite more than 20 years of equal opportunities and sex discrimination legislation, some 82 per cent of men and 86 per cent of females 'hate' to be subordinate to a woman. In Scotland the proportion rises to a staggering 95 per cent for both genders, according to Pitman Training, which conducted research among 1,000 employers and employees in the United Kingdom.

More positively, researchers discovered that we have become a nation of 'techno Brits' who crave the latest equipment and training on how to use it.

And experts predict that the typical office in 2010 will look more like a comfortably furnished private house with bright decor, workstations instead of desks and 'video conference meeting posts'.

The line between work and play will fade and the traditional nine-to-five working day will disappear, according to David Lewis, the psychologist whose consultancy prepared the report.

Some 82 per cent of men and 86 per cent of females 'hate' to be subordinate to a woman

Dr Lewis said that the high-stress office of today was based on a culture of long hours and little time for social activity, but that that environment was going to change.

'The office of 2010 will be a hi-tech haven, with gadgetry revolutionising the way we work. Pressure will be as much on the agenda as business. This will have a positive effect on family life as people will have increased leisure time and lower stress levels.'

Dr Lewis adds a word of warning however: 'No matter how advanced silicon intelligence becomes, we are still going to reserve our warmest, deepest and truest emotions for those clumsy, illogical and infuriating bipedal, carbon-based life-forms known as human beings. If that simple truth is ever forgotten the offices of tomorrow won't have any future at all.'

The present office environment gives little clue about the 'relaxing hi-tech haven' of the future, the report concedes. Nine out of ten employees claim that work pressures and stress have increased significantly over the past few years, Office staff work an average 44 hours a week and more than half work through their lunch hour.

© The Independent
May, 1998

Economic activity rates of mothers,* Great Britain, 1996 (%)

Mothers with children aged under five are the least likely to be in paid work. However, this group of women have seen the largest increase in labour market participation in recent years. Just over half of mothers with a child under five were in employment in 1996, including 16% who were working full-time.

Age of youngest child	Working full-time	Working part-time	Unemployed	Inactive
0-4	16%	33%	4%	47%
5-9	21%	41%	4%	32%
10 and over	30%	44%	3%	22%
All mothers	22%	39%	4%	35%

Source: General Household Survey (1998)

Go home for a long day at the office

Freedom from tyrannical bosses and petty rules, or a sad, lonely separation from workplace friends and colleagues? Penny Fox finds that working from home can be hard

There are some 3 million self-employed professionals who have set up their office within easy reach of their kitchen, whether it's the spare room, a shed at the bottom of the garden, or a specially converted loft space.

There are as many men as women and among their ranks are architects, accountants, journalists and consultants for almost anything you can think of. What they have in common is technology: screen-centred, modemed, e-mailed, linked to the Net. It's described as the freelance teleworking life and the language of the future: home-based nomads, telecottaging, out-sourcing, portfolio careers.

A new glossy targeted at people working from home or a small office, *SoHo Life*, will hit the newsstands in early June. Its publisher, Robin Johnson, says that his inspiration for launching the monthly magazine came from the massive array of technology available and the many benefits of working independently: 'Flexibility with more control, and an ability to plan your day according to your lifestyle. British Telecom has spent £30m saying "Why not change the way we work?" *SoHo Life* is going to show you how.'

The benefits of teleworking are numerous: waving goodbye to office politics, bureaucracy and commuting; gains in independence, flexibility and time with the family; choosing the work you want to do. But there is a price to pay: lack of financial cover for pensions, sickness and holidays; the feast-or-famine nature of much freelance work; the lack of company status and structure – and the lack of company.

Cary Cooper, professor of occupational psychology at the

The benefits of teleworking are numerous . . . but there is a price to pay

University of Manchester Institute of Science and Technology (Umist), has seen plenty of evidence of the social isolation that can affect the worker from home. 'I think it's a problem. We're hearing more and more from psychologists that changes in the nature of work are going to be quite profound in the next millennium: the future will not be office-based work. But people have an overwhelming social need. When they're not getting that social contact we see symptoms: some people get withdrawn, become almost housebound. They avoid the confrontation of other people; they start to get frightened; their social skills go off the boil a bit.'

Professor Cooper has observed that the freelance culture produces insecurity, with home workers often making many frantic telephone calls to all sorts of people, creating tele-contacts to establish a social context: 'But they want to be eyeball-to-eyeball, not tele-socialising. People who are more gregarious, who have high sociability levels and need to interact with others, are not going to find teleworking satisfying. Others who are task-driven, rather than relationship-driven, will function a heck of a lot better.'

The move from being an employee to being self-employed is similar to the transition from child to adult: an organisation sets rules and creates a hierarchy. You have to defer to people in a senior position, and you can become infantilised. When you're self-employed, suddenly there are no rules . . . There are no bosses, just clients. You have to be a grown-up.

For some, the transition is hard and depression can set in along with social isolation. Symptoms follow: headaches; endless minor colds; difficulties in sleeping and con-

ALTHOUGH HE'S STARTED WORKING FROM HOME HE STILL LIKES TO HAVE HIS MEETINGS

centrating; greater aggressiveness and anxiety; too much coffee or alcohol.

We may not like company rules, but the social side of office life and the demands placed on us daily by working relationships give us a wider dimension and another context to be ourselves in. The identity that work gives us, supported by peers and group membership, provides a sense of power and self-respect that is often not available through other activities. The cushions of company life – PAYE, company cars, pension and insurance schemes – take away some of the responsibilities that otherwise fall solidly on to the loaded, aching shoulders of the self-employed.

The people who pronounce themselves happiest with self-employment tend to be those who don't do it full time. They have some structure from part-time employment, and at other times the freedom to do more of what they choose. Professor Cooper would like to see the development of more flexible work practices but is concerned about our ability to cope healthily: 'The future is likely to be partly office, partly home. The technology is certainly there, but is the social technology around? Not at the moment.'

'My brain began to atrophy'

Heather Bayer became a 'sole trader' in management consultancy three years ago. She was 40 years old, married, with two children, and had previously been employed for eight years in the customer service division of a large company.

'It was really the idea of working from home that seemed so attractive, and the thought of being master of my own destiny. But it was like jumping off a mountain and hoping the parachute would open. I had no clear plans: I had a few contacts and, in retrospect, I should have had many more before taking the leap. It was difficult to keep the work going and make new contacts. Word of mouth created more work but it was a struggle.

'Sometimes the planning and control fell apart. I had to set my own goals and objectives and there was nobody to give me feedback.

There were times when I accepted far too much work and didn't plan how I would carry it out effectively. Too much work, and I would worry about letting people down; too little, and you worry about where the money is going to come from. Achieving the right balance was difficult.

Ten top tips for teleworkers

1. Discipline: put in place a set of rules and routines.
2. Money: create a strong relationship with your bank manager, accountant and financial adviser.
3. Work: learn to say no to work you don't want to do.
4. Work: if you're overloaded, contact clients and try to move deadlines.
5. Work: if you haven't got any, give yourself a structured break before launching back into sales mode.
6. Work: vary the types of work that you do and network with others in your field.
7. Social: make contact with other people in your area to break up the day.
8. Social: variety is important: spend time with people you don't like, not just with those who reinforce your own prejudices.
9. Social: take advantage of being in your area by getting involved with local organised activities or voluntary work.
10. Social and work: try to have meetings with clients. If the isolation is too great, consider renting an office away from home, sharing it with other self-employed people.

'I tend to leave everything to the last minute and work in panic mode, but working on your own doesn't lend itself to that sort of approach: you need to be structured. I started to get physical symptoms: my shoulder and neck muscles seized up. I was generally irritable and the family bore the brunt of any tension. You can't allow yourself to fall ill, you just have to work through it – and I think my health probably suffered. I ate hugely and probably put on a stone in weight because the fridge was there; and you don't get any exercise when you work at home. I found the lack of social contact really difficult and would spend hours on the phone just to have contact with people. My brain began to atrophy.

'For the business to carry on, I felt that having an office I could go to every day would achieve a number of outcomes: separating work from home and giving me a discipline. And if the business was to move forward, I was going to have to employ somebody full time. Five months ago I moved to our office. It's two and a half miles from home and I now get some exercise either cycling or walking to work. I employ two staff and run a busy office specialising in business skills training. Working from home wasn't as much fun as I thought it would be; having the office has made it all much easier to cope with. It's probably the best move I made since leaving full-time employment'

First published in The Independent May, 1998

Where time-management is child's play

Working from home takes self-discipline – but there are benefits, writes Sarah Jewell

After 15 years working full time in newspaper offices, I recently switched to working part time from home. With two small children to look after, and constant media admonishments about mothers working full time ringing in my ears, this seemed like an exciting opportunity for change. And whatever I am missing from office-based work is more than outweighed by the joy of being with my children. I love being able to pick up the baby and kiss her velvety cheeks whenever I want. I'm so glad I'm at home when my son has an accident at nursery school and returns sobbing, with an egg-sized lump on his forehead. I am thrilled by the delight on his face when he asks, 'are you working from home today, Mummy?'

But I hadn't anticipated the extent to which my whole rhythm of life would be affected.

The first thing I discovered was that, with no clear demarcation between home and work, the most important skills to develop are self-discipline and time-management. Instead of having a clearly defined beginning and end to the working day, with hours to fill in between, everything suddenly becomes compressed and compartmentalised, and the whole day is spent scurrying from one task to the next. Time for work has to be slotted in between doing the school run, the washing up, the laundry, the shopping and the cooking. As Melissa Benn says in her new book, *Madonna and Child*, 'women with children talk about time all the time: feeds, sleep, how many days they are at work, what they

manage or don't manage to do at home. Time torments them: time is a treasure.'

Time may be a torment, but far more torturing is the constant tidying up. Even a room full of journalists cannot create as much mess as a toddler, a baby and two or three of their little friends. It is so much easier to clear up the mess on your desk at the end of the day than it is to pick up mounds of plastic toys and sort out the accumulated debris of a day's play. One of the things I liked most about going out to work was coming home to a tidy house; now I work in

---

I hadn't anticipated the extent to which my whole rhythm of life would be affected

---

the study for an hour while the baby's asleep, knowing that when she wakes up I've still got to tackle the bomb site in the kitchen.

Lunch-time food is another big change. Beans on toast, boiled eggs and fish fingers . . . how I miss those delicious hot ciabatta sandwiches oozing with melted cheese and spicy salami, a plate of steaming canteen stodge – anything, in fact, that I haven't made myself. But after juggling the finances of working part time and paying for a commensurate amount of child care, eating out is a thing of the past.

Getting dressed up is pretty much a memory, too. Crisply ironed white shirts, pale linen trousers and neat little jackets hang forlornly in the wardrobe, while the same old jeans and baggy jumpers are paraded day after day. Mothers are not expected to look smart but there is something vaguely depressing about always slobbing about in old clothes, and I was delighted to see that even my brother-in-law, usually a real city slicker, had greasy hair and a baby-stained jumper after a week at home looking after his kids.

Of course, I don't see many men, apart from my husband, any more. That's one of the biggest changes, moving from a male-dominated world into a female one. Office banter and gossip are replaced by cosy teatime chats with other mums. But women with children are very supportive, and it is enjoyable to be warmly embraced into a child-centred world.

© *The Independent*
February, 1998

National Group on Homeworking guidance

How to look for homework and not lose money

Who we are & what we do

The National Group on Homeworking (NGH) is a campaign and lobbying organisation. We are the only national non-governmental organisation (NGO) in the UK working solely on homeworking issues. In addition to campaigning for improvements in the pay and conditions of existing homeworkers, we can provide advice and guidance to potential homeworkers on how to look for work to do at home.

NGH is a voluntary sector project which employs a small team of workers. We have limited resources and are currently funded by the National Lottery.

What we don't do

NGH is not an Employment Agency. Due to limited resources, we are not in a position to find homework for people. We do not hold lists of legitimate homeworking companies and cannot put you in touch with an employer. To our knowledge there is no such thing as a directory of companies offering genuine homework.

The purpose of this information

Although we are not an Employment Agency, in 1997 NGH was contacted by 1505 people enquiring about where they could find work to do at home. When looking for homework, or outwork as it's sometimes called, it is very important to be able to distinguish between genuine offers of work and misleading homeworking schemes, otherwise known as scams. Many people lose a great deal of money to unscrupulous companies advertising so-called homeworking opportunities every year. These bogus companies advertise largely in the press, in shop windows or put flyers through your letter box.

This information is intended as a guide to help you look for work to do at home and avoid being ripped off in the process!

Looking for homework – things to avoid

Having decided, for whatever reason, that you want to look for work to do at home, finding homework can often be a minefield! It may be tempting to reply to advertisements for homework you see advertised in the press or shop windows. Envelope addressing schemes are very common.

Recruitment schemes

Job opportunities for work from home mailing envelopes are often advertised in newsagents and Post Offices. You are asked to send off for details and then receive a request for a 'registration' fee to deter time wasters, or to cover 'admin costs'. Once the fee is sent, you are given instructions to place more adverts for homeworkers in other shops, often using your own address and the scheme organiser pays for any letters forwarded to them by you at about 30p per enquiry. The envelopes you will mail out – will be the s.a.e. sent in response to your advert. The company then writes to all the new victims requesting the fee for further details and so on and so on.

This is a typical example of a homeworking recruitment scam and NGH would always advise – never send money.

Envelope addressing

Like the recruitment scheme you will be expected to pay a fee. You will be expected to write out addresses by hand from lists provided (often copies of pages from telephone directories). This work is often rejected and you don't get paid and can't get a refund on your initial outlay.

Misleading homeworking schemes/scams

Like the recruitment scheme and the envelope addressing, there are other misleading homeworking schemes being advertised in both the local and national press and in shop windows all over the UK. Most common are directory scams and kit scams.

Directory scams

These ask you to send a fee (usually £15) in return for a list of companies offering work to homeworkers. You are encouraged to believe that the companies are reputable and are offering genuine work. What you actually receive for your money is just a list of photocopied sheets or a booklet of names and addresses or adverts for homework each asking a registration fee of anything between £10 and £200. To our knowledge there is no such thing as a directory of companies offering genuine homework.

Kit scams

These are often targeted at people who enjoy making things with their hands. They often have an arts & crafts-type emphasis, such as constructing lampshades or hand painting pictures/wall plaques or miniature clay cottages. You are invited to send money to a company in return for a kit. The kit can cost anything between £10 and £200. When the kit arrives it may have good materials in it, but no instructions on how to assemble the item, or it might be 2 sticks and a piece of fluff out of which you are expected to make a lampshade! Either way, it makes no difference, because whatever you send them they will reject the item on the basis that you have failed their quality standards and you will not be paid.

Many of these schemes can appear genuine. Their literature can look very professional and the rates of pay they offer very tempting. However, like trying to find any other kind of work you should never have to pay for homework. If a company is asking you for money upfront for homework, NGH would always advise never send money and have nothing to do with these schemes.

Remember – none of these schemes provide genuine types of homework. They are purely scams run by unscrupulous individuals who want to exploit your need to work at home.

For further information:

If you are in any doubt about the existence of a particular homeworking scheme/company and would like to find out more, then please contact The Companies Registration Office in Cardiff, Tel: 01222 380 801. For a small fee they can send you a named company's registration and incorporation details. However, this is no guarantee that the company is genuine or legitimate. NGH advises – avoid replying to companies using Post Office Box Numbers.

What to do if things go wrong

In 1997, NGH was contacted by 226 people reporting the names of companies whom they had fallen foul of. If you think you have lost money to a homeworking scheme you can telephone NGH to report the company and get further advice.

Freephone Homeworkers' Helpline tel: 0800 174 095 Monday – Friday (10am – 12.30pm and 1pm – 3.30pm). We can send you our *Practical Guide to Dealing with Misleading Adverts and Bogus homeworking schemes*. This booklet is free and will provide you with advice on how to proceed with trying to get your money back.

Some facts about homeworking

In most cases it is perfectly legal to work at home, providing that you are not causing a nuisance to your neighbours. Possible exceptions to this might be that some mortgage lenders or housing tenancy agreements prohibit you from working at home – so it is worth checking the terms before you start.

There are a wide variety of jobs that can be done in the home. Many people do not realise how many things are assembled, packaged, or processed by homeworkers. For example: academic gowns, Arran sweaters, bicycle parts, bingo ticket books, Christmas crackers, computer leads, draught excluders, data inputting, embroidery, felt tip pens, horse blankets, leggings, leaflets, medical supplies, pop socks, rag dolls, soldering wires, stringing labels, typing, umbrellas, word processing and selling financial services. These are just a few examples, there are hundreds of other items made by homeworkers.

How to find genuine work to do at home – NGH offers the following advice:

Finding homework can be difficult. You will rarely see homeworking jobs advertised in the Job Centre. Quite often, the only way you will hear about homework is from other people who are actually doing it. Somebody you know might know of a firm using homeworkers in your area. As most homework vacancies are usually passed on by word of mouth, it's always worth asking around. Ask your friends, neighbours or people you meet at the school gates.

Also – identify companies in your local area which might put work out to homeworkers. They will be listed in your local Yellow Pages or Thomson Directory. They will not mention 'homeworking' in their listing, but will be listed under the product or service they provide.

How homeworkers might be employed

Contract packers
These may use homeworkers to pack small items

Novelty or carnival manufacturers or firms making promotional items
These firms supply things such as keyrings, printed pens, or novelties for lucky bags. These could be assembled or packed at home

Clothing/knitwear manufacturers
These sometimes offer sewing work or knitting at home. These companies will usually want skilled workers and may want you to have your own machine.

Printed circuit manufacturers electronic components
These can be assembled at home.

These are only a few examples. There are hundreds of other goods which can be made, assembled or packed at home. Try to find work from a firm near to your home. This will make it easier to deliver and collect work.

What to do next

Once you have identified a company near to where you live:

- Call them up and ask if they ever employ homeworkers. The company should not charge you for this information.
- If they say 'yes', ask if they have any work at the moment.
- If they haven't, ask them whether they might have work in the future and if you can go on a waiting list.
- Tell them about any experience you may have.
- If the company does not employ homeworkers, ask if they know of other companies in the local area that do.

Telework

If you have a telephone and computer at home and you are considering doing telework, you could identify companies which tend to use teleworkers and operate telework systems. These tend to be in service industries such as banks, insurance companies and some local authority departments. Alternatively, contact the Telecottage Association (TCA) for further advice about working in this field. TCA Freephone 0800 616 008.

If you are considering homework as a route to self-employment, please contact the homeworkers' Helpline Tel: 0800 174 095 and ask for our *Guide to Self-Employment* booklet. These are free to homeworkers.

If you secure genuine work as a homeworker and require employment rights or welfare benefits advice please contact the homeworkers' Helpline and ask for a 'homeworkers' Fact Pack'. These are also free to homeworkers.

Remember:

- Never send money to a homeworking scheme.

- Ask friends and family if they know of any local companies who use homeworkers.
- Contact local companies direct about work.

NGH will endeavour to deal with your enquiries promptly and accurately and will treat all information given, with complete confidence. If you require a copy of our complaints and confidentiality procedures, please contact the NGH office: NGH, Office 26, 30-38 Dock Street, Leeds, LS10 1JF

If you secure genuine homework, you may wish to contact a local homeworking project which can give advice and guidance to homeworkers in their area.

• The above information is from the National Group on Homeworking (NGH). See page 41 for their address details.

© National Group on Homeworking, 1998

Homeworking

Don't be taken in by bogus job offers

Homeworking complaints

Although there are genuine jobs working at home, many are bogus. You should not have to pay to get work.

Never send money in advance to people or companies who claim they can offer you work at home.

These con tricks may start with an advert in a newspaper or a shop window, or on a local bus, or with a leaflet through your door.

Examples:

Adverts about addressing and stuffing envelopes. These are generally followed by a demand for a registration fee. All you get for your money is advice to place adverts like the one you saw. There is no real job. Just a scam to con you out of the registration fee.

Adverts asking for money for home assembly kits. These scams promise your money back and pay for making up the goods. You won't get money back. You will be told

that the goods are not up to standard or given some other excuse. The people behind the scheme never intended to pay you from the start.

If you have been the victim of a swindle like this, complain to your local Trading Standards Department. They are listed in phone books under Council.

If you see adverts in shop windows for what look like bogus schemes, complain to the shopkeeper. Show them this information.

If you see the advert in a magazine or a newspaper, you should complain to the Advertising Standards Authority. Cut the advertisement out and send it to them at No. 2 Torrington Place, London WC1E 7HW. Visit their web site: http://www.asa.org.uk to find out more about what advertisers must do to be legal, honest, decent and truthful.

For further information and advice contact: National Group on Homeworking Helpline 0800 174095.

Finding work

- Many homeworkers find work through word of mouth – ask friends, relatives or neighbours if they know of local employers looking for homeworkers. Approach local companies to find out whether they use homeworkers.
- Try to find work from a firm near you. It will be easier to collect and deliver work and sort out problems.
- Get recommendations from other homeworkers who work or who have worked for the company and have been paid.
- Find out more about a company before accepting work – you might be able to visit the premises.
- Ask at the local job centre.

Further copies of this information can be obtained by calling: 0870 1502 500.

© Crown Copyright 1999

Teleworking Britain

Executive summary

Who's teleworking?

The employees

- Thirty per cent of 'knowledge' employees are already teleworking or planning to do so soon. Applied to the general population, this amounts to 5.1% or 1.28 million workers are now teleworking, part or all of the time. When compared to the 1997 Labour Force Survey, where only four per cent or one million of the general working population teleworked (part or all of the time) – the growth in teleworking can be seen quite clearly.
- Men are more likely to telework – 34% of male respondents are teleworking or planning to do so versus 25% of female respondents. Women were more likely to claim they could not telework because their jobs require daily face-to-face dealings with staff or clients.

The employers

- Though Times Top 1000 companies are more likely than small-to-medium sized enterprises (SMEs) to be teleworking, sizeable proportions of both groups – 36% of SMEs and 59% of Top 1000 companies – are currently teleworking to some degree.
- That said, the penetration within teleworking companies is small, with the majority of respondents saying that only a few of their workers are currently teleworking.
- Nearly two-thirds of employers, both large and small, said that their companies do not encourage staff to telework.

Who could be teleworking?

The employees

- More than a third of current non-teleworkers said they would like to telework.
- Men were more likely than women to want to telework. Forty per cent of men stated a desire to do so versus 30% of women.

The employers

- Approximately one-third of employers (28% of Top 1000 and 31% of SME) also felt that secretarial and support staff were suitable for teleworking. Managers were seen as being the second most likely candidates.
- SME respondents were slightly more likely to believe that none of their staff were suitable for teleworking (21% versus 17% of Top 1000 respondents).
- The majority of current non-teleworking organisations are still resistant to the idea.

What's holding them back?

The employees

- Two-thirds of non-teleworkers said the primary reason for not teleworking was that it was not company policy.

The employers

'Against company policy' was also the main reason given by employers for resistance to teleworking, as stated by 43% of SMEs and 46% of Times Top 1000 companies.

- The findings suggest, not that a case has been made against teleworking, but simply that the teleworking proposition has not yet made it onto the boardroom agenda. Approximately one in four non-teleworking employers said they had never even thought about teleworking as an alternative.

Can teleworkers be trusted?

The employees

- Lack of trust on the part of employers is often cited as a reason that teleworking cannot work. The findings of this survey counter this argument. Three out of four employees believe that their employers would trust them to telework should they want to do so.
- Women were less likely to strongly agree that their employers would trust them. They didn't necessarily believe that they are mistrusted but were more likely to say that they just didn't know (20% versus only 6% of men).

Teleworking penetration within companies

Employers were asked what proportion of their workforce are currently teleworking. Unsurprisingly, given their increased financial and human resources, Times Top 1000 companies are more likely than small-to-medium seized enterprises (SMEs) to have at least a few employees teleworking.

Base: All employers (75 Top 1000/75 SME

Source: Mitel/MORI

The employers

- This belief in employee trustworthiness is borne out by employers, four out of five of whom say their staff can be trusted to telework properly. This figure includes employers who are not currently teleworking for whatever reason.

What are the benefits of teleworking?

The employees

- Teleworkers and non-teleworkers alike agreed that the key benefit of teleworking is greater job flexibility. This was deemed one of the top three benefits of the practice by 77% of teleworkers and 70% of non-teleworkers.
- Non-teleworkers were much more likely to perceive commuting savings (in terms of both time and money) as important – 70% named this as a top-three benefit versus only 42% of teleworkers.
- Teleworkers may well witness savings on commuting but are more likely to place greater value on enjoying a better lifestyle. Teleworkers were also less likely than non-teleworkers to view avoidance of office politics as a key benefit and more likely to value greater job satisfaction.

The employers

- Large companies were much more likely than SMEs to view major teleworking benefits in terms of building and maintaining a skilled workforce – either through retaining valuable staff (48% versus 29% of SMEs) or through recruiting from a wider pool of candidates where eligibility for employment is not limited by commuting distance or household commitments (40% versus 31% of SMEs).
- Significant proportions of both groups also cited improved competitiveness, increased productivity and improved competitiveness, improved quality of work as key teleworking benefits.

- SME respondents were more likely than their counterparts in larger organisations to see no benefits to teleworking (27% versus 19% of Top 1000 respondents).

What are the limitations to teleworking?

The employees

- Both teleworkers and non-teleworkers rated isolation (and consequent lack of teamwork) and difficulties in separating office and home life as the primary drawbacks to teleworking, although non-teleworkers voted for these in slightly greater numbers (84% and 73% versus 74% and 64% of teleworkers, respectively).
- Similar proportions (approximately 30%) of both current teleworkers and non-teleworkers also feared reduced opportunities for development/training.
- The greatest belief differences between the groups centred around information access and the perceptions of others. Teleworkers were much more likely to bemoan lack of access to information (48% versus 36% of non-teleworkers) and to worry about being thought less committed (36% versus 19%).

The employers

- Large companies were much more likely than SMEs to fear isolation of their staff and consequent damage to their corporate culture as a result of teleworking (47% versus 24% of SME respondents).

- SMEs were more likely to be worried about losing control of their teleworking workforce and its output (49% versus 36% of Times Top 1000 respondents).
- Other limitations, recognised by smaller numbers, were difficulty monitoring productivity, uneven standards of performance, technological problems, loss of confidentiality and falls in staff morale and loyalty.

What support is needed for teleworking?

The employees

- Company policy is the main issue preventing individuals from teleworking and company support is the main thing needed to get them started. Seventy-eight per cent of non-teleworkers who would like to telework said they require company support to telework. Logistical considerations – such as technical facilities – are also important, but space at home is not a major issue.

The employers

- Most teleworking companies do supply their teleworkers with the basic tools needed to work remotely – either a home or laptop PC and a mobile phone.
- Employers were less equipped with the components that can make teleworking really effective. Many of the fears faced by teleworking individuals – including isolation, lack of teamwork and inaccessibility of information – could be alleviated if proper systems, such as a teleworking intranet and remote home access, were put in place. Only a minority of employers have made such arrangements.
- Only one in ten respondents have drawn up a documented teleworking programme, including best practice. Six per cent have no formal teleworking arrangements whatsoever.
- The above is an extract from *Teleworking Britain – A study into the adoption and acceptance of teleworking within British business*, produced by Mitel.

© Mitel, 1998

Do high-flying jugglers really have it all?

Working mothers are sitting pretty in their executive chairs, says a new report. Labour Editor Barrie Clement is not convinced

According to Professor Heather Joshi of City University, London, while working-class women still struggle to combine work and family, their more upmarket sisters are finding it much easier. But should we run away with the idea that middle-class women have finally achieved equality in the workplace with men who take less responsibility for children? The answer is No. There may well be a disparity between the 'family-friendly' benefits enjoyed by those at the bottom of the heap and those much higher up, but you have to get to the very top – still a difficult business for women – before employers fall at your feet and minister to your family's every need.

Although lawyers advise companies to make benefits such as maternity leave open in equal measure to everyone in the organisation, less formal perks – such as occasionally working from home or rearranging schedules on an ad hoc basis to fit in with family life – are usually only on offer to the most senior people. There are also discreet bonuses available for the most highly trained to persuade them to come back to work after childbirth.

Some industrial sectors are clearly more family-friendly than others. Kirstie Axtens, of the pressure group Parents at Work, points out that the service industries such as banking and retailing tend to offer much better benefits than male-dominated sectors such as construction and engineering. Local authorities and government departments are traditionally also more helpful.

And the bigger the employer, the greater the chance that the needs of the working mother will be catered for. Such organisations inevitably have human resource departments which will champion such policies.

Medium-sized and smaller companies present a much bigger problem for parents at work.

Even in larger businesses, glossy brochures on equal opportunities policies are not necessarily translated into action at the sharp end. Many male middle managers are notorious for ignoring the lofty statements from the boardroom. Ms Axtens counsels that 'take-up' rates of available benefits will sometimes present a very different picture from that normally seen by the outside world.

The relatively enlightened corporate membership of Opportunity 2000 has led the way in the field of equal opportunities for the professional classes. Established in order to ensure that women smash their way through the glass ceiling, the company has elicited a whole

Teleworking revolution gathers pace

By Barrie Clement, Labour Editor

An extra 300,000 employees in Britain started to work from home over the past 12 months as part of the 'teleworking' revolution, says a poll published today.

But while high-tech companies are quickly shedding the 'bums-on-seats' approach to work, traditionally managed organisations are resisting the change, the MORI survey indicated. The poll, commissioned by information technology group Mitel, found that more than 5 per cent of the working population – some 1.3 million people – now spend part of their working week at home, compared with 1 million in the previous 12 months.

It was found that nearly one in three 'knowledge workers', especially in the financial sector, telecommunications, marketing, sales, professional services and media were now teleworking or planning to do so.

In a booklet published yesterday by the Confederation of British Industry and Mitel, it was argued that far more jobs could be partly performed at home with the help of an on-line computer, or even a lap-top and a modem. Strategic Workstyles, an Oxford consultancy, forecast that 25 per cent of jobs could be the subject of teleworking while the Telework, Telecottage and Telecentre Association estimates that the proportion could be as much as a half of all non-manual jobs.

However, in nine out of 10 businesses where employees are not already teleworking, managements say they have no plans to take up the option. 'Company policy' is cited as the reason.

Paul Butcher, managing director of Mitel, said that while Britain was way ahead of continental countries in switching to home-working, we were behind the US.

Mitel argues that there are substantial long-term financial advantages for companies, and environmental advantages for the community.

© The Independent
June , 1998

series of family-friendly policies from employers, albeit large ones. The vast majority of Opportunity 2000 members offer maternity leave above and beyond the call of legislation. Seven out of ten offer leave to new fathers, and five out of ten provide career breaks, adoptive parents' leave and advice on childcare facilities. Nearly a third have organised holiday play schemes.

There are still substantial problems to overcome, however. One of the most persistent is the long-hours culture that increasingly pervades the workplace. The man who stays behind after his normal working day is inevitably – and often superficially – regarded as a superior being. The woman who rushes home to look after the kids is not sufficiently committed, the argument goes. In some businesses – especially those which have been the victims of 'downsizing' – management may actually need people to work longer hours. Most working mothers would probably find it difficult to fulfil such a role.

There are also some professions where success is not best served by people taking long career breaks. Pat Corcoran, operations director at Opportunity 2000, gives the example of legal, scientific and technical jobs where the body of required knowledge can change rapidly. Ms Corcoran also suggests that adminis-trative posts are more susceptible to career breaks than management jobs. In the groves of academe, the don who produces regular and voluminous research over a long period is regarded as superior to a colleague who finds that family life impairs productivity. 'Success in some jobs can be a function of the amount of time put in,', says Ms Corcoran.

Perhaps the message is that while employers can help working mothers, the only real answer is that men should be encouraged or persuaded to take greater respons-ibility for their children.

© The Independent
January, 1998

Balancing work and family life

Women find balancing work and family life 'increasingly arduous', says survey

Women are finding the pressures of juggling work and domestic responsibilities increasingly arduous, and believe there has been a sharp deterioration in the quality of family life as a result, according to a women's magazine survey published yesterday.

Nearly three-quarters of those questioned said family life was now worse than in the past, while nine out of 10 felt the demands on women in balancing work and home life are greater than ever before.

The survey by *Prima*, the top-selling monthly women's magazine, involved analysing a random selection of 600 questionnaires out of thousands of responses from its 1.2 million readers, who cover a broad social spectrum.

The most serious problem, identified by 41 per cent of respondents, was the lack of time to satisfy the demands of both work and domestic life – with 22 per cent citing the cost of childcare and one in eight blaming the attitude of employers to working families.

Asked what they considered the best way for government to help working mothers, nearly a third said they wanted more state-sponsored

By Seumas Milne,
Labour Editor

nurseries, 21 per cent called for tax relief on child care and 19 per cent wanted higher child benefit. Two-thirds agreed that single mothers should be encouraged to work.

The survey is part of a campaign, Family 2000, launched by *Prima* last month along with an interview with Tony Blair, in which he said that families were under 'a lot more stress in the modern world'.

Two-thirds of *Prima* readers are under 45, 65 per cent are working women and 43 per cent have children under 15.

The survey results were welcomed yesterday by Lucy Lloyd, policy manager of Daycare Trust, the national child care campaign, who said they showed that 'the case for investing in childcare is stronger than ever'.

The Government needed to ensure that the £1 billion it was spending over the next three years on its national childcare strategy delivered 'high quality affordable services to all the families who need them'. As well as the Government's childcare programme, the intro-duction in October of the Working Time Directive regulating long hours, and the Employment Relations Bill – which gives an entitlement to unpaid parental leave and time off for domestic emergencies – are expected to have some impact on concerns identified in the survey.

The TUC's women's officer, Lucy Anderson, said yesterday that the organisation welcomed the Government's initiatives, but believed parental leave should be paid and that employers should be encouraged to help with childcare costs through tax concessions.

Mary Maguire of Unison, Britain's largest union – which has a large number of women members – called for the end of 'macho culture' in the workplace.

'We need to see the removal of the macho culture which demands very long working hours and attendance at meetings outside hours. That is a problem for men as well, but it particularly affects women because of the tag that goes on women that they are responsible for the home and children.'

© The Guardian
February, 1999

ADDITIONAL RESOURCES

You might like to contact the following organisations for further information. Due to the increasing cost of postage, many organisations cannot respond to enquiries unless they receive a stamped, addressed envelope.

Daycare Trust
380 Old Street
London, EC1V 9LT
Tel: 0171 739 2866
Fax: 0171 739 5579
E-mail: daycaretrust@londonweb.net
Promote affordable childcare for lone parents and people who want to go back to work. Produces publications.

Employment Policy Institute
Southbank House
Black Prince Road
London, SE1 7SJ
Tel: 0171 735 0777
Fax: 0171 793 8192
E-mail: epi@connect-2.co.uk
Promotes study and debate on all matters relating to employment, unemployment and training.

Family Policy Studies Centre
9 Tavistock Place
London, WC1H 9SN
Tel: 0171 388 5900
Fax: 0171 388 5600
E-mail: fpsc@mailbox.ulcc.ac.uk
Describes and analyses family trends and consider their implications for public policy; considers the impact of policies on families of different kinds. Publishes a wide range of materials including bulletins and reports.

Fawcett Society
5th Floor, 45 Beech Street
London, EC2Y 8AD
Tel: 0171 628 4441
Fax: 0171 628 2865
Campaigns for equality between women and men. Aims to influence parliament and public opinion to accept equal status for women in the home and public life, and equal educational and job opportunities.

Low Pay Unit
27-29 Amwell Street
London, EC1R 1TL
Tel: 0171 713 7616
Fax: 0171 713 7581
E-mail: lowpayunit@aol.com

Investigates low pay, poverty and related issues. Produces publications and employment rights advice. Please send an S.A.E.

Maternity Alliance
45 Beech Street
London, EC2P 2LX
Tel: 0171 588 8583
Fax: 0171 588 8584
E-mail: info@maternityalliance.org.uk
Publishes books, reports and information leaflets for parents-to-be, returners to work, and professionals on all aspects of maternity rights and services.

National Group on Homeworking (NGH)
Office 26
30-38 Dock Street
Leeds, LS10 1JF
Tel: 0113 245 4273
Tel: 0113 246 5616
E-mail: homeworking@gn.apc.org
The NGH is a research and lobbying group. It produces a useful set of factsheets on various aspects of homework. Please note that the NGH is not an employment agency and does not therefore keep name and address details of employers offering work. Also available is and *Employers Fact Pack* at £5.00. Helplines available are 0800 174 095 (English speakers) and 0800 028 0526 (Urdu and Punjabi).

New Ways to Work
309 Upper Street
London, N1 2TY
Tel: 0171 226 4026
Fax: 0171 354 2978
E-mail: nww@dircon.co.uk
Aims to change the culture in the workplace to give real freedom of choice to individuals who cannot or do not wish to work traditional work patterns. Produces a variety of information including a new series of nine factsheets on flexible work patterns.

Parents at Work
5th Floor, 45 Beech Street
London, EC2Y 8AD
Tel: 0171 628 3565
Fax: 0171 628 3591
The voice of working parents – campaigns to improve the quality of life for working parents and their children. Provides information and advice. Helpline: 0171 628 3581 open 24-hours Tuesday to Friday.

Public Concern at Work
Suite 306, 16 Baldwins Garden
London, EC1N 7RJ
Tel: 0171 404 6609
Fax: 0171 404 6576
E-mail: whistle@pcaw.demon.co.uk
Public Concern at Work is a legal advice centre and an independent charity. They were set up in the wake of the public enquiries into such disasters as Zeebrugge, Piper Alpha and the collapse of BCCI. Ask for their publications list.

The Industrial Society
Customer Centre
49 Calthorpe Road
Edgbaston
Birmingham, B15 1TH
Tel: 01870 400 1000
Fax: 01780 400 1099
E-mail: customercentre@indsoc.co.uk
The Society is a leading publisher of books, subscription reports and award winning video packs. Ask for their publications list.

Women Returners' Network (WRN)
344-354 Grays Inn Road
London, WC1X 2722
Tel: 0171 278 2900
Fax: 0171 278 2722
The Women Returners' Network (WRN) helps women back into fulfilling work after a career break. They have a helpline, publish resource sheets, produce a quarterly newsletter, hold conferences and seminars, and conduct research projects.

INDEX

The Internet has been likened to shopping in a supermarket without aisles. The press of a button on a Web browser can bring up thousands of sites but working your way through them to find what you want can involve long and frustrating on-line searches. And unfortunately many sites contain inaccurate, misleading or heavily biased information. Our researchers have therefore undertaken an extensive analysis to bring you a selection of quality Web site addresses.

★★★★★

Department of Health
http://www.doh.gov.uk/busguide.htm
The section, Day Care Services for Children, offers advice on The Children Act for those considering becoming childminders for working parents. The section, Employment of Children, provides a summary of the current legislation.

The Telecottage Association (TCA)
http://www.tca.org.uk
The TCA is Europe's largest organisation dedicated to the promotion of teleworking. Over 2,000 people have joined the TCA since it started in 1993 including individual teleworkers, companies, and telecottage/telecentre managers.

Childcare Search
http://www.opportunity-links.org.uk/ccsrmain.htm
To use the Childcare Search, there are three simple steps to work through.
1) Choose the type of childcare you want
2) Choose where to look for it
3) Carry out the search.
The search will take about a minute to complete.

European Telework Online
http://www.eto.org.uk
European Telework Online is the European and International focal point for information, news and discussion on telework, teletrade and teleco-operation.

ACKNOWLEDGEMENTS

The publisher is grateful for permission to reproduce the following material.

While every care has been taken to trace and acknowledge copyright, the publisher tenders its apology for any accidental infringement or where copyright has proved untraceable. The publisher would be pleased to come to a suitable arrangement in any such case with the rightful owner.

Chapter One: Coping at Work

I have seen the future and it doesn't work, First published in The Independent, May 1998, *The workplace revolution*, © The Guardian, January 1998, *Total usual weekly hours of work: by gender*, Spring 1998, © Labour Force Survey, Office for National Statistics, *Can this last?*, © The Independent, June 1998, *The great life/work debate*, © Ceridian Performance Partners, *Happy jobless laugh off the German work ethic*, © The Guardian, July 1998, *Careers turn heat on Cool Britannia*, © The Guardian, June 1998, *Office workers sinking under tide of technology*, © Telegraph Group Limited, London 1997, *All in a day's work*, © Gallup/Institute for the Future/San Jose State University study of Fortune 1000 companies, *Is this the end of nine to five?*, © The Daily Mail, May 1998, *Job insecurity leads to stress epidemic*, © The Guardian, January 1999.

Chapter Two: Young People and Work

New workers, © The Guardian, January 1999, *Speaking up, speaking out!*, © The Industrial Society, *For love or money*, © Family Policy Studies Centre, Autumn 1998, *Children 'not ready for work of tomorrow'*, © The Independent, April 1998, *What do young people want from work?*, © New Ways to Work, November 1998.

Chapter Three: Work and the Family

Juggling: it's not the way to relax, © The Independent, March 1998, *No question of multiple choice*, © The Guardian, January 1998, *Women in their prime as main breadwinners*, © The Daily Mail, November 1998, *New employers*, © The Guardian, January 1999, *Plight of the have-it-alls who miss family life*, © The Daily Mail, June, 1998, *A helping hand for women 'returners'*, © The Independent, May 1998, *Maternity rights*, © Crown copyright is reproduced with the permission of the Controller of Her Majesty's Stationery Office, *Main types of statutory maternity and paternity provision in the EU*, © Ruxton, S. (1996) Children in Europe, London: NCH Action for Children, *Parents at work*, © Parents at Work, *What future for the female boss?*, © The Independent, May 1998, *Economic activity rates of mothers, Great Britain, 1996*, © Crown copyright is reproduced with the permission of the Controller of Her Majesty's Stationery Office, *Go home for a long day at the office*, First published in The Independent, May 1998, *Where time-management is child's play*, © The Independent, February 1998, *National Group on Homeworking guidance*, © National Group on Homeworking, 1998, *Homeworking*, © Crown copyright is reproduced with the permission of the Controller of Her Majesty's Stationery Office, *Teleworking Britain*, © Mitel, 1998, *Teleworking penetration within companies*, © Mitel, 1998, *Do high-flying jugglers really have it all?*, © The Independent, January 1998, *Teleworking revolution gathers pace*, © The Independent, June 1998, *Balancing work and family life*, © The Guardian, February 1999.

Photographs and illustrations:

Pages 1, 2, 5, 8, 11, 14, 16, 18, 20, 21, 24, 27, 33: Simon Kneebone, pages 6, 12, 15, 32, 35: Pumpkin House, pages 9, 26: Katherine Fleming, page 31: Ken Pyne.

Craig Donnellan
Cambridge
April, 1999